TOM
LAND

THE SURVIVORS

BY HENRY RASMUSSEN

THE SUR

One hectic day last spring, I was packing my camera equipment. I placed the big Mamiya RB 67 in its foam rubber compartment, and then the 50mm wide-angle lens and the 180mm telephoto lens. With the magnifying hood in place, and the pistol-grip, and all the other accessories, plus a king-size bag of Kodak Ektachrome film, the cases were filled to the limit.

The next morning I arrived in London, the starting point for an expedition that would in a challenging endeavor combine my professional interest in photography with my nostalgic interest in cars. This task would take me all over England and the Continent, in search of the fabulous cars of yesterday and their enthusiast owners of today. My assignment was to record in pictures and words the fascinating stories of the greatest among "The Survivors."

In order to uncover the reasons for my romantic involvement with cars, I have to go back to my childhood. Back to the years in Sweden and Norway, just after World War Two, when the cars were coming out of their war-time hiding places. The visual images from my youthful experiences with cars show up sharp and clear. They are like filmstrips reaching far back, connecting me with the past.

In the earliest of these visions I find myself in the front seat of a vintage Model A Ford, creeping up the steep and winding roads outside Oslo. The occasion was a family picnic. Grandfather was at the wheel. I can see how he constantly checked the engine

temperature, and how we had to stop halfway up the hill to let it cool off, and how on the way down he was not concerned with the engine anymore, but with the brakes.

Later visions show a Citroen on a trip to "Lands End" in Southern Norway, and a dark blue Buick belonging to a doctor. I can see the Buick and the Ford side by side in the cool darkness of the garage, smelling of rubber and gasoline.

The events that formed a highpoint took place in Sweden a few years later. The setting in my vision is a green countryside with fields and forests. It was a warm and sunlit summer without worries. Now and then my friends and I would hear the distant roar of a racing engine. We knew what it was and jumped on our bikes, sped down the hill to the road and let the bikes fall in the grass beside the banking. Then we waited to catch a glimpse of the blue and gray monster that would soon appear on the unpaved country road with a whirling dust cloud behind it.

After it had passed we would stand there in silence, with sand-chewing teeth and blinking eyes, experiencing a climactic feeling that would not be repeated until the next time the car would race by.

But one thing troubled us. We could not find out the name of the arrogant-looking open two-seater. One time we caught it going through a hairpin curve, but it still went too fast for us to read the name badge. It remained a mystery and a source of endless discussions, until at the close of the summer I happened to spot it parked outside the bank in a nearby town. The letters on the radiator formed a name that just had to be the most romantic ever given to a car. It was a Lea-Francis.

Now, many years later, I had the opportunity to see the priceless collector's cars I had only heard of before. I saw them as they were, and they were not over-polished, or over-restored, or over-protected. The European philosophy of owning an old car was different from the American. The cars were in constant use. They were driven hard; the way they were built to be used. And they had that beautiful patina which comes with age.

Seeing the cars through the camera was a very good way to get acquainted with their form and

features. I had to move far away to see the cars in the landscape, and very close to take in the details. A photographer can inject into a picture his own special way of looking at objects, depending on the angles and lenses he chooses, the lighting and the background. On the pages of this book the viewer will see the cars portrayed in my own subjective way.

This assignment would not have succeeded without the valuable cooperation of the car owners. They represent an exclusive group of genuine enthusiasts. Survivors in their own right, they were holding on to values and qualities of a bygone life style. Some of them had owned their cars for twenty, thirty, and even forty years. They were willing to spend all the time necessary to make my endeavors successful. They did this without commercial interest; just for personal satisfaction.

In addition to thanking these generous owners, I also want to express my appreciation to the many who shared with me their knowledge and contacts; among them famous automobile historian Michael Sedgewick, the staff at Lord Montagu's Motor Museum, and Richard and Trisha Pilkington, owners of Totnes Automobile Museum.

After many years I had now added new links to my chain of car experiences. But would there ever again be a car as good as my first love, the Lea-Francis? Only time can tell as the memories mature.

Carl Benz and Gottfried Daimler were both pioneers in the automobile industry. In 1887 the gasoline engine was placed in production by Daimler and that same year Benz patented his three-wheel car. As early as 1901 the "Mercedes" model was introduced by Daimler and named after the daughter of one of the financiers. In 1926 the two car-makers merged. Ferdinand Porsche, who in 1921 had taken over as technical director at Daimler, now started an ambitious development program that led to the magnificent Mercedes-Benz sportscars and racing machines of the Twenties and Thirties.

In 1936 the 540 K appeared, directly based on the 380 K and 500 K. Its 8-cylinder engine developed 180 hp with the supercharger engaged. This gave the heavy (5,800-pound) car a top speed of 110 mph; not as impressive as the SSK of ten years earlier. But what the 540 K lacked in handling and performance was compensated by its arrogant elegance. It was the favorite of the super-rich in the years preceding World War Two.

The 1939 540 K Spezial Roadster, shown here for the first time was Hitler's choice when he wanted to make friends with Stalin. But the gift was not well received, and the car was given to one of Stalin's generals as a staffcar. In 1962 a Swedish translator, Alf Johansson, found it and managed to smuggle it out of Russia. The recently discovered "survivor" was photographed in Sweden on a beautiful summer evening.

With Bentley representing the typical British sportscar, Rally the French, and BMW the German, Alfa-Romeo was the natural choice as a representative of the Italian vintage sportscar. Guiseppe Merosi developed the first Alfa in 1910. The company was reorganized in 1919 by Nicola Romeo, and the first important racing victory came in 1923 at Targa Florio, Italy.

About that time the gifted designer, Vittorio Jano, joined Alfa-Romeo as chief designer. He was first responsible for the successful P 2 racecar, which captured the World Championship in 1925. Then, a few years later, he created one of the most beautiful and functional vintage sportscars of all time—the 1750—a favorite among all ages of car enthusiasts. With drivers like Novulari, Campari, and Varzi behind the wheel, it racked up victories on the circuits all over Europe.

The car featured here is a 1750 Grand Sport from 1929, with an exceptionally attractive early Zagato body. Only available on special order, no more than 370 were ever built. It had a six-cylinder supercharged engine giving a power output of 85 hp, and a top speed of 90 mph. This vintage classic is owned by an Alfa-Romeo expert, Roy Slater. It was photographed close to his home outside Milan, Italy, on the same hill where the Alfa-Romeos were first test-driven almost fifty years ago.

MERCEDES-BENZ 1939

ALFA-ROMEO 1929

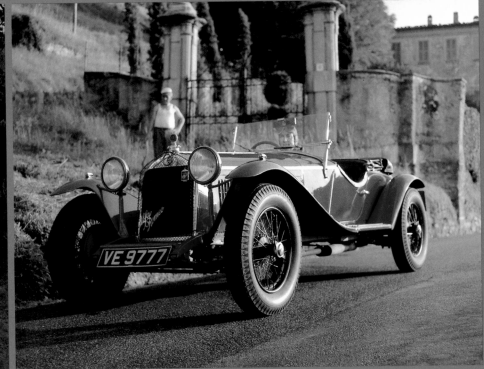

The first Sunbeam appeared in 1899, manufactured by a bicycle company in Wolverhampton, England. Sunbeams recorded scores of victories on the early racing circuits, and had already set many speed-records before World War One. After the war Sunbeam merged with Talbot, still retaining its separate identity. Fifty-one world speed-records were set in 1922, and in 1923 and 1924 came victories in the French and Spanish Grand Prix events. In 1925 the world speed-record was attacked again and an impressive 150 mph reached. Two years later, a twin-engined 1,000 hp Sunbeam finally passed the 200 mph-limit on Daytona Beach, placing the new record at 204 mph.

In 1925 a three-litre model was introduced, designed to compete with the successful Bentleys. Even though it didn't do too well on the race tracks, it was highly respected in the sportscar version. The car shown here has a one-of-a-kind body by Gordon England, built on the three-litre Le Mans chassis. Its six-cylinder engine with dual overhead cams produced 90 hp at 3,800 rpm. This unique Sunbeam was photographed in Farnham, a quaint little town in Southern England.

Edward Armitage ordered his Sunbeam in 1926, and used it until the outbreak of World War Two, when it was stored and then forgotten. Some years ago his daughter and her husband found it and felt it was time to resurrect the beautiful vintage classic.

Bayerische Motoren Werke had been building motorcycles since 1919, when in 1928 they decided it was time to try the automobile market. Rights to produce the English Austin Seven under license were obtained, and the BMW-version was named Dixie. By 1932 Fritz Fiedler had designed a car that became the first true BMW. In 1936 he had refined his design into a new two-litre model which was the beginning of the famous 328, introduced the following year. This revolutionary automobile was considered the best all-around sports car available on the prewar market. It came second in the 1939 Le Mans and third in the 1940 Mille Miglia.

The 328 shown here belongs to well-known rally driver, Betty Haig. She picked it up in Munich in 1938 when it was brand new. It is still in her garage in a beautiful 16th-century house in Southern England. She often takes it for a fast drive on the narrow roads of the English countryside. It was photographed on one of these memorable occasions.

This streamlined silver BMW has a six-cylinder, three-carburetor engine, developing 80 hp at 4,600 rpm. It gives the 1,800-pound car a top speed of well over 100 mph and it accelerates from 0 to 60 in 11 seconds.

SUNBEAM 1926

BMW 1938

Hispano-Suiza was the leading French luxury car during the Twenties and Thirties. The first model was shown in 1904, then manufactured in Barcelona, Spain. Its creator was the Swiss engineer, Marc Birkigt, who became one of the most famous car designers of all time.

Hispano-Suiza was called "The Car of Kings," originating from the 1911 model, "Alfonso XIII," which was named after its most enthusiastic admirer, the King of Spain. In the early Twenties, production was concentrated to Paris. In spite of its luxury image, Hispano-Suiza was also a great race car. In 1928 a Hispano-Suiza beat a Stutz to win the Indianapolis 500.

The model considered by many to be the most magnificent production car ever made was the V-12, introduced in 1931. Shown here is a 68 Bis from 1934. The Bis refers to the eleven-litre engine volume. Very few were sold due to the unreachable price tag. The black stove-enamelled engine developed 220 hp and gave the car an impressive acceleration: from 0 to 60 in 12 seconds, and a top speed of over 100 mph.

The Hispano-Suiza was photographed at a 17th-century castle outside Lucerne, Switzerland. The owner of this extremely rare car, Yves-Jaques Rey-Millet, found it in his grandfather's boathouse on the French Atlantic coast. It had been hidden there under rotting boats to escape the eyes of the Nazis during World War Two.

A French engineer with the impressive name of Eugéne Affoward Asniére, started in the early Twenties to build the Rally automobile in his small shop outside Paris. In the beginning it was only a little more than a cyclecar, powered by a Harley-Davidson motorcycle engine. Later it was fitted with a more potent 4-cylinder engine and the body was made wider and lower. Together with cars like Salmson, Lombard, and Amilcar, Rally was the archetype of the French vintage sportscar.

In 1926 a supercharged version was shown at the Paris Salon. Next year a small series was produced; some estimate that only 14 or 16 of this model were built. The cars performed especially well in rallies, scoring victories in Tour de France and also in Rallye Feminine with the famous Madame Leblanc behind the wheel.

The 1928 Rally Grand Sport shown here is one of only three still known to exist in Europe. It has a supercharged 1,100 cc Chapui-Dornier engine delivering 70 hp, giving the lightweight car a top speed of close to 110 mph. The price in 1928 was 42,900 francs. Swiss textile designer Albin Machaz bought it for 500 francs in 1950. For two decades he didn't know what a rare car he owned, until he recently began to restore it, and the Rally was uncovered from layers of postwar body-modifications. It was photographed outside St. Gallen, not far from Bodensee, Switzerland.

HISPANO-SUIZA 1934

RALLY 1928

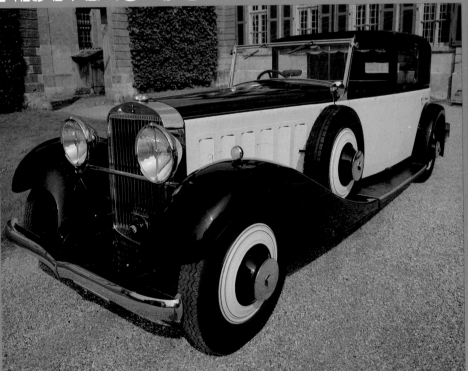

In 1905 the French engineer Louis Delage started his own motor company with only three workmen in his shop. A few years later he had 350 men working for him, and reached a production of 1,000 cars annually. Successes on the race tracks were equally impressive. In 1914 two Delages dared to cross the Atlantic to enter the Indianapolis 500, finishing first and third.

Delage faced financial problems during the depression, and was bought out in 1935. The new owners continued to build Delage's cars, but retired the creator himself. From then on, some experts say, Delages were never the same, although today the flashy cars, with their extravagant bodystyles, are among the most sought after by collectors all over the world.

The car featured here is a DB 120 from 1938. It has a straight eight-cylinder engine, and an electro-magnetic gearbox. When tested by Autocar Magazine it was felt that "in spite of the long bonnet, the driver feels able to handle the car confidently at first acquaintance." It accelerated from 0 to 60 in 17 seconds. Top speed on the quarter mile was 98 mph.

Nothing is known about the history of this car during World War Two, but some years afterwards it appeared at Grabers, the famous Swiss coach builder. Pierre Strinati saw it on his way back from a cave expedition to the Swiss Alps. He bought it on the spot. The Delage was photographed early one summer morning on the shores of Lake Geneva, Switzerland.

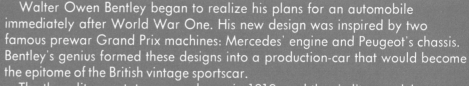

Walter Owen Bentley began to realize his plans for an automobile immediately after World War One. His new design was inspired by two famous prewar Grand Prix machines: Mercedes' engine and Peugeot's chassis. Bentley's genius formed these designs into a production-car that would become the epitome of the British vintage sportscar.

The three-litre prototype was shown in 1919, and the six-litre model was introduced in 1926. This was the famous Speed Six. It won the 24-hour race at Le Mans in 1929, and repeated its victory the year after. As much as Bentley's talent for engineering was the reason for his success, his lack of talent in financial matters caused his failure. In 1931 he went bankrupt. That year marks the last of the "real" Bentleys.

The car featured here is a Speed Six from 1929; only 129 were built that year. Its six-cylinder engine produced 180 hp at 3,000 rpm. The top speed was close to 90 mph. Many years later, one of these rare cars fell in the hands of Bob May. It was supposed to be his retirement toy. But he couldn't just sit still and admire his new possession. He had to drive it. He began to compete in vintage races, and today he has driven the car on three continents. The Bentley and its speed-loving owner were photographed on a cloudy afternoon outside Abingdon, a three-hour drive south from London.

DELAGE 1938

BENTLEY 1929

When Frederick Henry Royce acquired an automobile for his personal use in 1903, he was so disappointed in the unreliable and unrefined construction that he decided to build his own car. One year later it was ready for introduction. When the wealthy Charles Stuart Rolls saw it he was very impressed. He immediately accepted an offer to become part of the new company. This partnership was destined to produce an automobile that today still is the standard by which cars are measured for comfort and quality.

The famous "Silver Ghost" was introduced in 1906. For two decades it was the favorite of English Gentlemen as well as Kings and Maharajas. In 1925 it was time for "Phantom I". It had a new six-cylinder engine believed to develop 100 hp. The exact figure was not known—since 1912 it was Rolls-Royce policy not to reveal such data.

The car shown here is a two-seater "Doctor's Coupe" by the famous coach builder Barker. It was photographed on the grounds of Westover Farms in Southern England. The owner, Adrian Liddell, fell in love with the yellow Rolls-Royce at an auction many years ago. But the bidding went too high for his budget, so he left disappointed. Later, when he came home, the owner was waiting for him. The high bidder had not been able to come up with the money, so Mr. Liddell was able to buy it at his own price.

Ettore Bugatti was the artist among classic car makers, creating automobiles that would go down in history as the most legendary of all. He was born in Italy, where he first studied to become a sculptor. But after building his first car in 1899, he had found another way to express his artistic talent. In 1907 he started a factory of his own in Molsheim, close to the French border in Southwestern Germany. The new borders established after World War One placed the Bugatti factory in France.

Many great models rolled out from Molsheim in the years to come; powerful race cars like Type 35, and elegant luxury cars like Type 41 "Royale." They were raced by famous drivers like Tchaikowsky, Dreyfus, and Chiron, and owned by glamorous people like the King of Rumania.

The car featured here is a Type 57 S "Atalante" from 1937. Its handpolished satin-finish alloy engine developed 185 hp and gave the car a top speed of 125 mph. It was the fastest unsupercharged road-car money could buy. Among the more notable racing victories was the 1937 24-hour Le Mans race.

During World War Two this car was hidden somewhere in Belgium. Afterwards it was restored, and later shipped to the United States. Today it has returned to its homeland, France, and is owned by the well-known Bugatti enthusiast, André Binda. The last of the famous Bugattis was photographed on the Paul Ricard race track Northeast of Marseilles, France.

ROLLS-ROYCE 1926

BUGATTI 1937

Major Antonio Lago, an accomplished engineer in his own right, was the manager of the Darracq factory outside Paris when the multi-national Sunbeam-Talbot-Darracq-conglomerate fell apart, in 1935. He managed to acquire the French facilities and the following year he introduced Talbot-Lago. The same year his cars took the two first places in the Tourist Trophy Race at Donington Park, England, and in 1936 the three first places in the Sportscar Grand Prix at Montlhéry, France.

After the war a four-litre engine was developed for Formula One competition. The 1950 Le Mans race was won with Louis Rosier behind the wheel. The production model was fitted with the Grand Prix engine, but in this version it developed 170 hp, giving the car a top speed of over 110 mph.

The Talbot pictured here is a 1948 Lago Record with a Drophead Coupe body built by the factory. In spite of its postwar production date, it is a prewar design, engine and styling being a direct continuation of the 1939 car. This magnificent machine is photographed with the famous skyline of Monte Carlo as a backdrop. The car was restored by a team of aviation mechanics between 1960 and 1963. Today the Swiss owner, Count de Wurstemberger, keeps it at his Riviera Villa in Menton, France.

In 1923 Cecil Kimber assembled a car from various available components and called the result MG, after the name of his service shop, Morris Garages. The car did well in trials and races, and he continued to build cars. But the big sales success didn't come until 1929, with the Midget. Then followed the famous TA, TB, and TC, which were responsible for triggering the sports car interest in United States.

Many different models were made, from family sedans to speed-record breakers. One of the most rare ones was the K 3 Magnette, a six-cylinder race car. With its supercharger it could reach speeds of over 120 mph.

In 1947, only a few years after the end of World War Two, a Swiss gentleman calling himself "Herwe" purchased one of the few remaining Magnettes. He had some modifications done to adapt the car to his stiff leg. Then he set out to conquer the hearts of Swiss racing enthusiasts, by winning his first race, beating all the postwar cars with his fourteen-year-old MG.

This "survivor" was photographed outside the picturesque town of Totnes in Southern England. There the MG enjoys its old age in a small Motor Museum on Steamer Quai. Once in a while it is let loose to compete in vintage races, where all it shows the opponents is the beautifully pointed tail. The owner is still the mystical "Herwe."

TALBOT-LAGO 1948

MG 1934

Different parts of the automobile filled different practical purposes. They were first of all designed to perform in their designated areas, but at the same time be pleasing to the eye. The design of details became an important sales point and reflected trends in art and fashion. On the following pages, some of the more visible objects are grouped together: name badges, wheels, instrument gauges, headlights, engines, steering wheels, and other details. The badge of Rolls-Royce is the oldest and most well-known among the ones featured on this spread. It was first used on the "Silver Ghost" in 1906. In 1933 the red color was changed to black for esthetic reasons. By coincidence it also came to mark the death of Sir Henry Royce. The dark spots on the legendary Bugatti badge are not defects. They are bugs from one of the owner's recent trips to Austria and Greece. BMW and Rally are both typical examples of their art periods. The BMW typifies the functionalistic simplicity dominating German design immediately after World War One. The Rally badge reflects the elegant French Art Deco style, growing in the Twenties and blooming in the Thirties.

Spokes and hub form a decorative pattern in the large close-up to the left. The wheel belongs to the MG Magnette raced by "Herwe" on Swiss circuits immediately after World War Two. Knock-off nuts were used to enable the pit-crew to make the quick wheel-changes so critical for the outcome of a race. The wire-wheel was typical for the British sports car. On the Continent, especially in Germany, solid, die-stamped wheels were popular. Betty Haig's BMW was originally fitted with solid-type rims which were later exchanged for light-weight ones, partially shown in the close-up to the right. These wheels had twelve weight-saving holes along the edge of the rim.

Four famous racing engines are featured on these pages. The large picture to the right shows the six-cylinder power source of the BMW. The three carburetors form a row of hungry mouths, ready for their oxygen. The picture in the middle, further to the right, shows the impressive-looking six-cylinder Sunbeam engine. This was developed especially for Le Mans racing, and expected to be potent enough to compete with the successful Bentleys. But the victories didn't come, mainly due to chassis shortcomings, and few units of this three-litre version were made. Below the picture of the Sunbeam is the beautiful Alfa Romeo engine. Fitted with supercharger, it developed 85 hp and was one of the most successful of all the vintage racing engines. Note the graceful design of the exhaust manifolds, with their decorative cooling fins. The picture to the far right reveals what the Bentley has under its long bonnet. This Speed Six has three SU carburetors and was modified with a McKenzie manifold. The owner, Bob May, competed with his Bentley in the Ghent Speed Trials in Holland. On the flying kilometer he recorded an impressive 101 mph, which gave him first place in the vintage class. The club magazine later reported that the car "went very well, lights blazing and a lovely throaty exhaust noise—a real achievement and a great credit to car and driver."

Drivers of vintage cars enjoyed sights like the ones in the close-up shots on this spread. To a sports car enthusiast on a Sunday drive, the tachometer was just a pleasing and decorative instrument, most of the time. But to the racing driver it was of utmost importance. By keeping an eye on the tachometer he could, in spite of deafening noise from engines around him on the track, determine when to shift and see his exact speed before going into the curves. The pictures show several instruments, beginning with the tachometer belonging to the Delage, at the right. The yellow field tells the driver when the engine is reaching top performance, but also warns him not to exceed this limit. The next picture shows the speedometer of Stalin's Mercedes. This car could reach speeds in excess of 175 kmph with the supercharger engaged. The elegant beauty of the Mercedes dashboard was fully realized when its lights were turned on as in the photo. Wood was not good enough as a setting, it had to be mother-of-pearl! The last picture shows the large, no-nonsense tachometer of the MG Magnette.

One of the most characteristic features of the vintage car was the headlights. Their size and position would determine the "facial expression" of the automobile. They could be placed high as on many of the British cars, or low and close together as was often the case with French cars of this period. The headlights would receive the most loving attention from their owners, who kept them polished and spotless. Shown in the large close-up to the left is the impressive headlight of the Hispano-Suiza, a piece of art in itself. The pictures to the right are both of the Rolls-Royce. The world-famous radiator is reflected in the curved back of its own headlight. The setting sun creates a soft tone, also coloring the photo further to the left. This light was operated by the driver and used to cast light on areas that could not be reached by the headlights.

Simplicity characterizes the BMW dashboard shown to the left. A crude, masculine look was achieved by using an all-metal construction; the steering wheel in the picture was added later. A sharp contrast to the BMW is the rich wooden elegance of the Delage pictured above. Rolls-Royce, to the right, still had controls in the center of the steering wheel; a leftover from early models. The picture to the far right shows the unusual design of the MG steering wheel, which later would become so familiar to American sports car enthusiasts.

Shown on this spread are some of the decorative details that made vintage cars look so beautiful and interesting. Pictured to the far left is an unusual object from the Rolls-Royce; an air intake in the form of a ship's ventilator. A warm summer day could be a painful experience for the driver's feet, when the heat from the engine would pass right through the uninsulated divider wall. On such a day, it was a relief to have the ventilator provide a breeze of cool air. The large close-up in the middle shows the delicately curved exhaust pipes of the Delage. This feature gave the car a most elegant and powerful appearance. The dramatically flared tail end of the MG Magnette's exhaust system is pictured to the left. It was developed for racing on the Brooklands circuit outside London. As the city grew closer, the surrounding population began to complain about the noise from the race cars, so they were fitted with this system that cut down on the sound level.

Cars and drivers form inseparable units in the pictures on these pages. The reflection in the mirror of the BMW above belongs to famous race driver, Betty Haig, wearing the same hat she wore in the early rallies and hill climbs on the Continent. Sitting behind the wheel in Stalin's Mercedes is the proud owner, Alf Johansson, while behind him the Swedish scenery glows in the late afternoon light. To the right of this picture is Fred Mance, in the Sunbeam that belonged to his father-in-law since it was new in 1926. The large photo on the right-hand page shows Adrian Liddell in the yellow Rolls-Royce inspecting the growing crop on his 1,000-acre farm in Southern England; an impressive sight that brings back memories of the good old days of motoring.

MERCEDES-BENZ

TO STALIN FROM HITLER WITH LOVE

It was the summer of 1962. Alf Johanson, a Swede working in Russia as a translator, closed the door of his office at Moscow Radio. Downstairs, his Russian friend Boris was waiting in his car, a Zaporosjetz, ready to take him out of the city. It was necessary to use Boris' car because foreigners could not travel more than forty kilometers outside Moscow, and this time Alf had to go further. Besides, Boris was needed for another reason. He was the only one who knew where to find the general's summer house.

Alf was tense today. He was close to the end of his long search. Almost two years had passed since he first heard about the Big Black Mercedes. According to the rumors it was the car that Hitler had given to Stalin in 1939 to convince the Russian dictator of his sincere friendship. But Stalin had become furious when he saw the gift; to him it was the very symbol of capitalist decadence. He didn't want to have anything to do with the Mercedes, and since it was considered unwise to return the gift, it was given to one of his generals as a staff car. That was all Alf had been able to find out. Until he met Boris.

Alf had been very cautious when he asked around for the car. He knew he was under observation. All foreigners were. And this kind of curiosity could easily be misunderstood. He had discovered where the microphones in his apartment were located. They didn't bother him much anymore; when he wanted to talk, he just turned the radio up loud.

After a long chain of contacts he had finally found Boris. And Boris knew where the general's summer house was—the general who was supposed to own the Big Black Mercedes.

They drove out of the city on the broad tree-lined boulevards, through the concrete suburbs, and into the soft green belt of birch forest that surrounds Moscow. After more than an hour, they left the road. A dirt track took them deeper into the forest, and

after awhile they saw cottages among the trees. Boris hesitated, then turned in through the gate to a small house built of crude timber. He got out of the car and found someone to talk to. He came back. No, the general had died recently, but the son was there. Yes, the car was there too.

That day, Alf saw the Big Black Mercedes for the first time. It had been parked behind the cottage under some fir trees. A heavy army tarp had been thrown over it. He still remembers the dark shadows of the trees and all the brown needles on the tarp. And how, when he removed it, the first thing he saw was that the radiator star was missing. He opened the bonnet with the same feeling he had when opening a church door. The engine was massive, heavy-looking, and gray. The chromed exhaust pipes emerged like the horns of a water buffalo. He found the brass identification plate: Baujahr 1939, Auftragsnummer 317029. He checked the piece of paper in his pocket where he had jotted down the information from the factory. It was the right car. A 540 K Special Roadster, the only one built with that body style. His mind immediately began to tackle the question of how the car could become his.

It was thirteen years later, in Sweden, on an unpredictable day. Unpredictable because you could not tell if it was going to rain or not. The summer rains come so quickly in Scandinavia. You see the dark gray mass of clouds in the distance, and the rain-like watercolor brushstrokes connecting the clouds with the ground. You see all this still far away, and then before you know, it's right above you.

Alf and the American photographer were looking out through the open garage doors, until the rain passed. They were ready to take the Mercedes out to be photographed. They would go west from Ljungby, into the countryside, where the lakes, fields and forests fit into each other like pieces of a puzzle. It would be the first time since 1967 that Alf had taken a good test run. Since getting the car out of Russia, he had been restoring the body. The engine he had not touched. As far as he could tell, it had never been opened. In Russia he had driven the Mercedes almost daily, without any trouble. He had taken it to the
(Continued overleaf)

Two of the major political figures of the Second World War, Hitler and Stalin, shown in the photographs to the left, played important roles in the drama surrounding the Mercedes. In the fall of 1939 Germany and Russia were negotiating a peace treaty, and Hitler felt it was a good idea to oil the wheels by presenting this magnificent automobile to Stalin. The picture above was taken outside Moscow, where Alf Johansson discovered the car in 1962. The man in the checkered shirt is the son of one of Stalin's generals, the one who used the Mercedes as a staff car during the war.

Black and chrome give Stalin's Mercedes the sophisticated look appropriate for a statesman's car. Pictured to the right is the elegant interior made from genuine materials like leather, steel and mother-of-pearl. A comparison between driver and car in the side view (above) gives an idea of the gigantic proportions of the heavyweight roadster. Swedish summer clouds are reflected in the flowing surface of the Mercedes' tail end in the picture further to the right. It had three hidden compartments. The first space behind the driver contained the hood, the second covered the rumble seat, the third concealed a spare wheel. The large photograph on the right-hand side captures the arrogant-looking Mercedes front, with its beaming headlights.

Black Sea resorts on his vacations, and on other trips that he had been allowed to make. Altogether he had driven 20,000 kilometers in Russia. He still had the Russian spark plugs in it. Alf opened the bonnet and showed them to the American photographer. They had no brand-name, only some letters he couldn't understand.

"I think we have to put in new plugs. It runs only on five cylinders now. I hope new plugs will do it." Alf closed the bonnet carefully. "The rain has stopped, let's see how it works."

They drove the Mercedes down to the shore; as close to the water as they dared. The lake narrowed and a bridge led over to the other side. The American photographer waved to a passing motorboat, and asked to be taken out on the lake. He wanted to get a shot of the car from out on the lake. Now he was out there in the boat, leaning over the side, making small waves so the sky would be reflected in the many facets of the water, as he took the pictures. On the ground glass of his camera, he saw the Mercedes on shore. He saw the big round fenders, the recessed radiator, and the headlights. The beautiful headlights.

"Turn on the lights!" the American photographer called to Alf on the shore. He looked at the sun. The headlights would show up nicely against the soft evening sky. He shot three rolls from the boat and five more on the shore.

When they were ready to go back, they went up the hill to the road, and then after a few kilometers they turned onto the highway.

"It took two months before I could finally buy it. The general's son was willing to sell, but that wasn't enough. In Russia you just don't go out and buy a car; you have to wait in line and a car will someday be allotted to you. The chances that the Mercedes would be allotted to me were, of course, none. So I had to beat the system somehow. After trying regular channels without any luck, I finally, with help from my contacts at Moscow Radio, got an audience with the minister of commerce, Sjumanskij. I talked about the importance of preserving a cultural treasure, and told him that the car was now deteriorating. He said that he would see what he could do, and after a second visit it was all cleared up. But the most difficult part was yet to come.

"I now owned the Mercedes, but it wasn't really mine if I had to leave it in Russia forever. I had to come up with some way of getting it out of the country. Applying for an export license would never work. In my mind I devised all kinds of wild plans. One included rebuilding the front to make it look like a Russian car. Another meant taking it apart and shipping it out with machine parts. But all the plans seemed too risky. If it was discovered the Mercedes would be lost and I would end up in Siberia. I finally decided to take a very simple approach. I would drive out of the country as a tourist, pretending that I would come back again.

"When I arrived at the last Border Control before Finland, I had a hard time hiding my nervousness. The border officials all gathered around the car to look and ask questions. I acted as casual as possible. The fact that I spoke fluent Russian made it easier, and they let me pass, all my papers being in order. In Finland I could finally relax, knowing that the Mercedes was really mine. Later, I heard that the Russian authorities had found out what had happened. There had been some investigation and then changes in the law. Now it can't be done anymore."

Well, out on the highway Alf wanted to try the supercharger. He hadn't used it since he drove home from Russia. He pressed the accelerator to the floor but nothing happened. He did it again, and again. Suddenly there was a violent kick in the back, a sound of sirens, and the car was thrown forward in a wind-splitting thrust. Resting in the middle of all this brute power was the illuminated dashboard, made from mother-of-pearl. An almost feminine creation, like a jewelry box on a lady's make-up table. The American photographer glanced at the speedometer. It showed one hundred and forty. He looked out to the side of the road where the trees were rushing by. It didn't seem that fast, he thought. The heavy rain clouds were gathering above again. Only a stripe of orange showed where the sun was setting.

The American photographer turned to Alf and shouted over the screaming supercharger, "Don't you think Stalin tried it out in secret, some dark night?"

"I'm sure he did," Alf smiled, "nobody can resist this kind of capitalist decadence."

Alf Johansson, in the picture on the left-hand page, poses beside his prize possession, parked on a typical Moscow boulevard. The apartment where he lived during his stay in Russia was located a few blocks away from where this photograph was taken. He used the Mercedes on several long trips to the Black Sea Coast, and it always attracted much attention whenever he stopped. Russian generals can be seen among the curious passers-by in the picture above. Sometimes Alf brought the car to Moscow Radio, where he worked, and it became a special treat among the dignitaries to be taken for a ride in the eye-catching beauty.

ALFA-ROMEO

SAME HILL FIFTY YEARS LATER

The American photographer had called Saturday night from Genoa. There had been no answer. Then he had called from Milan. He called several times, but there had still not been any answer. The next day he had driven to Monza to see the famous race track there, and the automobile museum. But it was closed. Then he called again from Monza. This time Mister Slater's wife had answered. Yes, they owned an Alfa Romeo. Yes, Mister Slater would be home after six in the evening. Yes, maybe they could let him see the car, but he would have to call back later.

The American photographer had tried for three days to find anyone who knew anything about vintage Alfa Romeos. He wanted to photograph a 1750, or a 2300, or a 2900 in the country where it had been made. That's why he was so anxious to find one here in Italy. He had tried all the addresses and phone numbers that people in England and Switzerland had given him. But there had been no answer anywhere. And the streets of Milan had been deserted. He had never seen a big city so empty. All the people he talked to would throw up their hands in resignation and say "vacazione," which he supposed meant

vacation. Evidently all of Italy was closed for holiday at this time of the year.

He had heard of a 2900 in Trieste. But that was too far to go. Besides, it was all taken apart for restoration. Now he had finally made contact with Mister Slater, an Englishman, who had lived in Italy for a number of years and owned a 1750. This was the model most sought after by collectors, although the American photographer himself had always favored the extravagant late prewar forms of the 2900.

Around seven the same evening, he had called Mister Slater from the Village Cafe in Cirnusco Lambordini, north of Milan, on the way to Lecco. While he waited, he watched the men play billiards. Outside, there was heavy rain and thunder. It sounded like it was moving around in circles just above their heads. When he wasn't watching at the tables, he stood in front of the window, waiting to see the lightning and enjoying the way the rain came down on the trees, the tile roofs and the cobble stones.

When he called this time, Mister Slater was home. No, it was difficult to meet tonight because they had guests for dinner, but yes, since he had tried so hard

The 1930 racing season was a tremendous success for the Alfa-Romeo 1750, with victories in the Belgian Grand Prix and Targa Florio, Italy. It was also a great year for Alfa's star driver, Tazio Nuvolari. He added to the success by winning both the Mille Miglia in Italy and the Tourist Trophy Race in Ireland with his 1750. Two of his fellow Alfa drivers, Campari and Varzi, are pictured beside their cars in the larger photograph on the left-hand page. The picture below it shows Nuvolari ready to flash his famous victory smile. In the photograph above, he displays his winning style on the rain-drenched Ards circuit, near Belfast, Ireland.

for so long without success, Mister Slater would see him at eight.

When the American photographer knocked at the door to Mister Slater's house, he didn't know that he had misunderstood the arrangements. Since the Slaters had dinner guests, they were supposed to have met in the cafe in the village instead. So Mister Slater opened the door with a surprised expression and said, "I don't think we have had the pleasure . . ." They looked at each other for a moment, and then they both understood the misunderstanding. They squeezed together around the dinner table and made room for another guest. And they served him goulash with rice, bread and wine. It was all very embarrassing, but later they forgot about it and Mister Slater started to talk.

"My parents moved to London in the thirties, I don't remember exactly when, but I must have been thirteen or fourteen. It didn't take me long to find some friends. All we talked about in those days were cars. We went to Brooklands and saw them race, Raymond Mace and the other great race drivers. We built model cars, pushing them around, imitating the sound of the engines they didn't have. A little later we started with the real ones. We bought them old and cheap. Ten pounds, maybe, was all we paid. We took them apart, fixed what was wrong, and put them together again. You learn an awful lot about cars that way. We had the front-wheel-drive Alvis, the Bebe Peugeot, the Amilcar . . ."

Mister Slater leaned forward with the bottle of wine and filled everybody's glasses. The bottle had no label, and the American photographer thought to himself that it must be a local wine.

"What great friends I had there. It's funny how many kept up the interest in cars. Johnny Green, for instance, he writes about Bentley. Lawrie Dalton writes about Rolls Royce. Tony Ellis, he became the secretary of the Lotus Club, and Jack, Jack Hyslop, he became secretary of the Bugatti Owners' Club. I have written two books myself, maybe you have seen them, both on Alfa Romeo. I've had fifteen of them. Loved them all. Yes, it was great to grow up with these chaps. And Colin Chapman, he built his first car just
(Continued overleaf)

Birthplace of the vintage Alfa Romeo racing machines: Milan, in northern Italy. They were speed tested on the Monza circuit twenty miles outside the city, but for more severe conditions the factory drivers took their cars to Monte Veccio further north. The pictures on this spread were all taken on that same hill, where almost fifty years earlier the bright red sports cars came speeding up the steep and winding road, with the sound of their superchargers echoing in the surrounding valleys. The setting, with its vineyards and villages, was as paradoxical as it was picturesque. The photograph to the right shows owner Roy Slater, resting in his car. The evening sun, reflected in the rear view mirror, casts a ray of light on his classic profile.

a few blocks away from where I lived. I saw the beginnings. Who else did I know?''

The question was directed to his wife, but the ladies were discussing Italian cooking. He turned to the American photographer again.

"But there were bad things too. The Sundays were bad. Then I had to go to church with my parents, and in the afternoon I had to stay in my room. What made it so bad was that I knew the other boys were down at the Cappa Racetrack in Somerset, driving the cars we had fixed up. Every Sunday was like that.''

Mister Slater was silent. He looked like he had more to tell, but instead he stood up and motioned to the American photographer to follow. They went down the stairs to the garage. There were five or six Alfas packed in there. Two of them were red vintage models. One was a 6C 1500, the other one was the 6C 1750. They walked over to it.

"They started to build these in 1929. It was actually shown the first time at the Motor Show in Rome in January that year. This is one of the earliest, you can see it on the trim here; in the beginning they used aluminum, so that's how you know it. Only about 370 were ever built. Mine is a Zagato-bodied Gran Sport with supercharger. The engine puts out about 85 horsepower. Top speed is over 90 miles per hour.''

Mister Slater went over to the workbench, opened a wooden box, and pulled out an old driving cap of dark brown leather and a pair of old racing glasses. He put on the cap, and then the glasses. He placed them on his forehead, then lowered them over his eyes. Finally he let them hang loose around his neck. He looked at the American photographer imitating the famous smile of Novulari; the Italian race driver hero.

"Novulari used to race these cars, you know. He won the 1930 Mille Miglia in one. He was 38 years old then, a magnificent driver. There is a story about him and how he won the Mille Miglia that year. He had been second to Varzi during most of the race, but he drove like mad the last couple of hours and finally, in the early morning mist, he had seen the tail lights of Varzi's car in front of him. He switched off his own lights and sneaked up behind. Just two miles before the finish, he passed the surprised Varzi and managed to keep away from him and win. I can

appreciate what these chaps went through, I drove Mille Miglia myself. That, of course, was the commemoration race in 1968. It was fifty years since they started it.''

By now the others had come down too, and they were all standing around the car. Mister Slater turned to his wife.

"Do you remember our big incident at Mille Miglia? In the rain? We were getting close to Bologna, when it started to pour down so bad that all the cars stopped. Even the police ran for protection. But we continued, remember? We hadn't fitted the hood in those days, and we drove on until we got to the checkpoint, Il Papagallo, the restaurant, you know. We were wet to the skin, our pockets were full of water, and we asked if there was any way we could dry off before we ate, but there wasn't, so we had to eat all wet like that. Do you remember what we had? It was Pappadelle al Lepre, I think. Anyway, it tasted delicious!''

They were all laughing and having a good time. It was getting pretty late, and they began to feel tired from all the food and wine. It was decided that tomorrow, when Mister Slater came back from Milan in the evening, they would drive to Monte Veccio. This was the mountain, only a few kilometers away, where the Alfa Romeo test drivers used to take their cars to give them a real run. That was in the late Twenties. Sometimes they would run them so hard that when they got to the top, the engines were boiling. Mister Slater and the others started up the stairs. They were all pretty tired by now. Tomorrow, the American photographer would get his pictures of the Alfa Romeo on the same hill where they used to drive them in the early days. He was satisfied.

When a vintage race was arranged in 1968 to
commemorate the first Mille Miglia, fifty years earlier,
Roy Slater was among those honored with an
invitation. With his wife as co-driver, in the upper
picture, to the left, he is greeted on the finishing line
by Mille Miglia's famous starter, Renzo Castagneto.
The smiling enthusiast in cap and glasses is Guidotti,
who was Nuvolari's co-driver in the 1930 victory
car. The race offered a variety of weather conditions,
as can be seen in the pictures to the lower left
and above.

SUNBEAM

IN MEMORY OF A LOST BRIDE

The train came to a halt with the brakes making the high-pitched sound that Mister Armitage always felt as a quick, icy pain in his teeth. He stepped down on the platform, walked through the iron gate, and was absorbed by the crowd at Waterloo Station in London. He stopped for a moment to buy the Daily Telegraph, gave the man who held out a hand his two pence and continued towards the exit. The morning sun broke through the soot-covered glass ceiling as he looked up at the big clock hanging there high above him. It was a few minutes after ten.

Edward Armitage was a man in his early thirties. Sudden circumstances had placed him in charge of the family business. He had a degree in bridge designing from Cambridge. Even though he was not constructing bridges now, as the family firm specialized in parts for the automotive industry, he was very well suited for his job. In fact he had already developed a new system for the automatic lubrication of cars. The interest in automobiles ran in the family. Around the turn of the century, they had manufactured the well-known Pilgrim Cars. His fascination for motoring also showed in another way not so well liked by the older members of the family—he used to race sports cars at Brooklands almost every weekend.

As usual there was a long line of people waiting for cabs outside the station. Mister Armitage couldn't see himself wasting valuable time. He walked around the corner and started up the street. After a few blocks he found a cab.

"Good morning!"

"Good morning, Sir. And it's a lovely one, isn't it? Where to, Sir?"

"The Bath Club in St. James', please."

He leaned back in the black leather seat and opened his newspaper. It was Monday, the 3rd of May, 1926. He scanned the main headlines. Rail Strike Order. State of Emergency. He turned to page eleven and began to read the news summary.

"The nation is faced with the calamity of a general strike at midnight tonight. The services threatened are railways, trams, buses, and all other transport." He wondered how he would get back to Farnham tonight; maybe he would have to stay in London. He read on.

"Electricity and gas, printing trades, metal and heavy chemicals, iron and steel industry are also threatened." This meant problems for Mister Armitage. The rest of the article didn't relieve his worries.

"It has been stated that there is no need for anxiety on the part of the public with regard to the supply of milk and other foodstuffs." He didn't care much about whether he had milk to drink, but whether he could make his deliveries on time, or not. All this could have created unpleasant thoughts in the mind of Mister Armitage. But it didn't. He was in a good mood. He turned to the back page.

"Autos for sale. Sunbeam, three-litre sports four-seater, 1926. Mileage 4,000. Practically new. Special opportunity and real bargain for 975 pounds."

The cab turned the corner at Oxford Street and St. James. Mister Armitage asked the driver to wait a few minutes while he made a phone call at the club. He needed to talk to his fiancée Margery about some purchases he had promised to take care of during his stay in London. They were engaged to be married, and the wedding would take place in three weeks. He had saved money to buy a house, and they had been looking at several already, but hadn't made a final decision. Mister Armitage thought about the house they would get, about furniture, about his bride. It was all very nice, and he was still in a good mood as he entered the Bath Club.

Ten minutes later the cab driver saw Mister Armitage come out through the door. He was a different man; something had happened. The face was pale. The eyes looking far away. The driver waited a moment, then decided next that he needed to know.

(Continued overleaf)

Sunbeam-owner Edward Armitage was an avid supporter of Brooklands, with its airfield and race track; he was familiar with both, as a spectator and competitor. The picture on the left-hand page was found in one of the photo albums he left at his death in 1969, and it is assumed that he was the man in the cockpit, since he was an experienced pilot. In the picture to the left, the photographer captured the Sunbeam parked in front of the family home at Tilford. It was taken in the late Twenties. Of even earlier date is the photograph above showing Mr. Armitage as a young man, dressed in midshipman's uniform.

Sunbeam, with its many speed records, was a name on every motor enthusiast's lips. The sportiest of the production models was the three-litre version. These cars were only built on order, reaching a total of 250; they were fitted with custom bodies by various coach builders. Edward Armitage's car was built by Gordon England, who was interviewed recently at the age of 83. He remembered this particular car and referred to it as his masterpiece. Notice the fenders in the picture to the left, the way they turn with the wheels. Another fashionable feature was the pointed tail shown in the picture to the right. The coach builder's bill came to 515 pounds; his invoice is still in the owner's possession. Cost of the chassis was 950 pounds, making it a total of 1465 pounds—quite a sum of money in 1926. A careful study of the license plate reveals a crack in the glass. When Edward Armitage's son-in-law noticed the flaw, he wanted to correct it. But he discovered that the number was hand painted on the back of the glass, so he decided to keep it as it was, crack and all—an example of the enthusiast's desire to keep his car in original shape.

"Where to, Sir?"

"Just drive around the block a couple of times, will you!"

Mister Armitage searched within himself for a reason. Why had she broken off the engagement? What had gone wrong? Was it something he had done? Or not done? Was there anything he could do now? The cab went many times around the block, and finally he understood. He knew that this was all for the best. Thinking back, he understood. He was not happy. He was sad. But he felt satisfied that he understood, and that he had made a decision. He leaned forward to the driver.

"Go to Wembley. To the Palace of Industry."

Mister Armitage paid for the cab. He stood for a moment in front of the building, listening to the sound of the cab engine disappear. He looked up at the sign on the wall above the windows. Gordon England Limited, Coach Builders. He went up the stairs and entered a large room with three enormous drafting tables. The walls were filled with drawings of cars, some in full scale. A young man looked up from one of the tables and walked towards him.

"I'm looking for Gordon England."

"That's me. What can I do for you?"

"Can you build me a special body for a Sunbeam?"

"A Sunbeam you say? Do you have the chassis?"

"Yes, I can get one of the new ones designed for Le Mans, the three-litre with twin overhead cams."

"Excellent. We should be able to do something very nice on that. Come with me out to the shop, I would like to show you how we work, then we can come back and discuss the details of the design."

They went downstairs and came out in a large hall, where a dozen workmen were occupied with completing the different steps in assembling the bodies.

"Look over here: we make the body panels out of aluminum, and we attach them to a wood frame. Light and strong. And then we attach the body to the chassis at only three points. Here, here and one on the back there. We call it a floating body. It doesn't touch at any other point. Here you see the bodies we make for Austin; Triumphs are over there and, in the corner, Morris Oxford." They went back upstairs to the large room with the drafting tables. Mister

England took a pencil and started to sketch.

"I have had something like this in mind for some time now. But I wanted to save it for a special occasion. I want to put all the best ideas into one creation. How do you like these lines? Too advanced?"

"No, no, I like them. But may be the back end could slope a little more? What do you think?"

The two men were leaning over the drawing table. They were discussing the louvres on the bonnet, and the location of the spare wheels. Mister Armitage was unaware of the fact that he was not thinking about his lost bride anymore.

Forty-nine years later, the American photographer came to see the result of the two men's work. He saw the beautiful Sunbeam at Brooklands Racetrack, where the members of the Brooklands Society gathered for their Annual Reunion. He met Mister Armitage's daughter and her husband, who told him all about the car. How Mister Armitage used it until the war started in 1939. How it was left in the garage, and how they found it after her father died, the engine in a corner all in pieces. They told him how they had stripped the whole body and repainted it in the original colors. How they had put the engine together again, and how excited they had been when it started at the first try. They also told him about Mister Armitage's broken engagement, and how he had taken the money he had saved to buy his bride a house, and bought a car for it instead.

And the Sunbeam was there—still going strong.

At the beginning of the century, Edward Armitage's father was the manufacturer of Pilgrim cars, shown outside the factory in the picture to the upper left. The picture above reveals the silhouette of the Sunbeam as it was photographed in the coachbuilder's showroom in 1926. Notice the unusual boat tail and the aerodynamic shape of the foot board. Mr. Armitage's daughter, Imelda, and her husband, Fred Mance, relax in front of their precious possession in the picture to the lower left. The occasion was a vintage rally, where the couple captured the award for Pride of Ownership.

REFLECTIONS IN A REAR VIEW MIRROR

The woman walked ahead of him with long, deliberate steps. Their feet made crunching noises in the loose gravel covering the courtyard of the charming old house where she lived. She was dressed in a sky-blue sweater, and wore slacks in almost the same blue shade. Her hair was gray. The American photographer found it hard to believe that this woman, with her soft and peaceful manner, was the famous racedriver Betty Haig, the winner of numerous rallies and hill climbs, and the last woman to drive the ultimate endurance test, the twenty-four-hour race at Le Mans. It was difficult to understand how she could produce the toughness it took to master the powerful racing machines used in these events. But the scores of trophies and plaques filling her study certainly proved that she was very good at the occupation she had chosen. Just as they passed a rosetree climbing up the withering stone wall, she turned to him, and her eyes were as blue as her sweater.

"This is where I keep it," she said, and pushed the heavy, black garage door to the side.

As the door opened a rectangle of sunlight fell on the silver body of a BMW 328. The American photographer immediately recognized the rounded forms of the famous prewar classic, as it became fully visible. Hanging on the wall behind the car he could see the red number plate from the Monte Carlo Rally. Beside it hung the blue plate from the Alpine Trial. It had number thirty-six painted on it. There were tools and engine parts spread out on the workbench to the right. The floor had a pattern of dark circles from years of oil leaks. Today it was swept clean, and fresh sawdust was sprinkled over the darkest spots. Together they pushed the BMW out in the sun.

"I picked it up myself in Munich. That was in June of 1939. The BMW was gray then; it wasn't available in silver. My plan was to export it to Hungary, where they didn't charge import duty on new cars. I had to do it this way because I couldn't afford to pay the 700 pounds the car would have cost in England. Exported to Hungary, it cost me only 300 pounds. I say "only" because it was quite a saving, but back then it was still a lot of money. I remember arriving in Munich very late in the evening. Already early next

morning the Hungarian agent, Mister Rauchbauer, was waiting outside the hotel. There were two cars to be driven to Hungary; my gray one and another BMW 328 that was white. The trade plates were taped to the curved fronts, and we immediately started on our long journey. The Austrian border was crossed with a minimum of formalities. It was sparsely manned, probably because of the 'Anschluss' that had just taken place. 'Anschluss' was a term used by the Nazis, referring to the German takeover of Austria. Described in a more realistic way, the army of the Third Reich had simply marched into their neighbor country, crushing all resistance in a powerful and quick maneuver. We travelled on the new Autobahn, along the winding banks of the river Danube. The two lanes lay deserted; only occasionally did we meet or pass another car. Quite a contrast to the Autobahn were the narrow and dusty roads in Hungary. We drove through primitive villages, where the only vehicles we saw were horse-drawn carts. The same evening we arrived in the Hungarian capital, Budapest.''

She walked around the car, placed one hand on the steering wheel, and moved it slightly from side to side. There was hardly any slack.

''I still marvel today at the incredibly light and direct steering. I suppose I realized that the 328 was a car of the future. A car that would be unbeatable by any other contemporary sports car in its class. I also realized that I had to learn a new driving technique. The BMW had nothing of the 'snaking' so typical for British sports cars of the same period. It had a new 'one piece' feeling. During my stay in Budapest it was run in, and I became more and more familiar with my new car. I was delighted, to say the least. The factory had advised me not to exceed 4,500 revs, and never let it drop below 2,500 in intermediate gears. With the light flywheel, a sudden snatch could damage the transmission. Before I left Budapest, the BMW had its 500-mile service.''

She squeezed down behind the wheel. Her movements were maybe not quite so graceful as they used to be, but they were done with the elegance that comes with years of practice. She picked up the dark blue driving hat with the large sunshade. She *(Continued overleaf)*

The BMW 328, in the upper left picture, is held up at the checkpoint on the border between Germany and Austria in 1938. Notice the Hungarian export plates taped to the front. In the lower left picture the BMW charges through a curve at the 1947 Pool Speed Trials in England. The photograph above was taken as the BMW was being sent out on the track of the 1948 Rheineck-Walzenhausen Hill Climb in Switzerland. Owner Betty Haig was the spectators' favorite and captured a very honorable third place.

Shellingford House, a cluster of beautiful old buildings dating back to the 16th century, provides a peaceful background for Betty Haig's powerful-looking BMW. With its well-known license plate, it is still a popular competitor in hill climbs and vintage races. Nowadays it lives a more secluded life than before, resting in the garage seen behind the car, in the large picture to the left. A closer examination of the front reveals the unique badge of the Hungarian Automobile Club—a memento from the BMW's prewar days, when it was registered in Budapest.

pulled it over her head, tucking in the curls of gray hair that had remained outside. As she began to fasten the strap under her chin she continued to tell her story. The American photographer changed to a wide-angle lens and interrupted her only with occasional questions.

"As the summer of 1939 went on, it seemed like the last months of peace were running out. I felt that this might be the last opportunity to travel on the Continent, so I decided to go to Spain. At that time the bitter fighting of the civil war had just come to an end. From the mechanical viewpoint it was a trouble-free journey. From a psychological viewpoint it was the opposite. My exciting experiences ranged from a river-crossing on an army lorry because the bridge was bombed, to a border-crossing with guns pointing into the car. On the journey back, my return was blocked by the French army making its way to the Maginot Line. Eventually I reached the Newhaven channel boat, and there I learned that the first British forces had already landed. Many people returning before me were unable to get their cars on the passenger-packed boats and had been forced to leave them on the quai. Among other cars I saw a brand new Delahaye abandoned there. I was fortunate in being so late, and the crew was able to crane-lift the little BMW onto deck. Shortly afterwards it was laid up in the safety of a Sussex barn, where it came to rest for six long years."

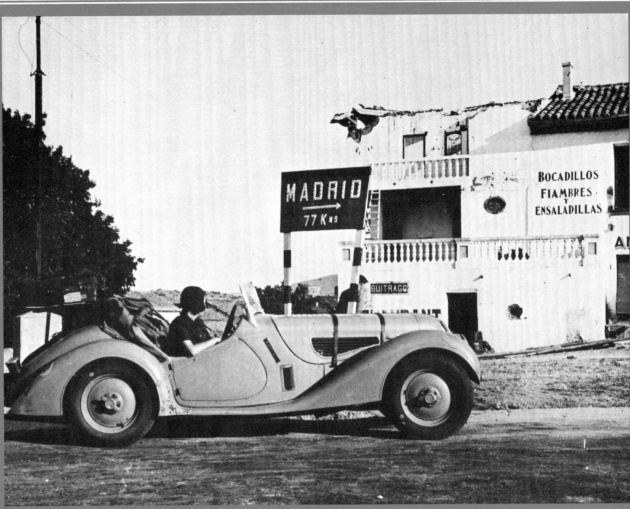

She drove out through the gate, turned first to the right, and then to the left at the intersection in the village. The American photographer sat beside her in the narrow cockpit. He held the heavy camera in a steady grip, ready to record the action. A rapid sequence of shifting took them out on open road. On both sides of the car, the British summer fields were rushing by in quickly changing shades of green. The driver and her passenger were completely surrounded by the hypnotizing sounds of the swirling wind and the six-cylinder engine at 3,500 revs. For a short moment he saw her face in the rear view mirror. Her eyes were fixed on the road, but they were also looking at something very far away. Suddenly she started to talk, without turning to him. He could hardly hear her words over the thundering engine.

"I remember the hill climb in Rheineck-Walzenhausen in Northern Switzerland. They sent us away a couple of minutes apart. It was a dangerous course because of the different road surfaces. You started on cobblestones; you went straight out of the village and then you turned sharp to the left as you rounded the hotel. You were still on cobblestones, but in the middle of the curve you were suddenly on asphalt! The cars had slid around there and lost oil. It was rather slippery. You had to shift down to second, brake a little, and then give full power just at the right point. I started well prepared that time. I had spent a fortnight in the village before the race, practically living on the hill. I had five or six other BMWs to compete with plus various other fast cars.

The other BMW drivers took their spare wheels off to lighten their cars, but I felt that roadworthiness was more important, so I kept mine on for better weight distribution. I also had SU carburetors, while the others had Solex. For whatever reason, I came in third, which I was very pleased with. When I reached the top, Jaques who had gone up several cars ahead of me, was waiting with his Swedish friend. When I passed over the finish line they lifted their glasses of apple cider in salute."

The American photographer saw her face in the mirror again. Her mouth had a little smile. Her eyes were slightly squinted, looking far away. She was back in 1948. He pressed the shutter release on his camera.

These two pictures were taken by owner Betty Haig during her 1939 journey through a Spain scarred by the fighting of the Civil War. The unique photographs show the BMW with its conspicuous luggage rack and primitive hood. The burned, bombed and barbed-wire countryside forms an almost surrealistic background. Taking pictures was prohibited, so the film was hidden under a floor board in the car. Miss Haig managed to return to England just before the outbreak of the Second World War made it impossible to travel by car in Europe. She arrived at the English Channel just as the first British troops landed on French soil.

IN THE CORNER BEHIND THE ROTTING BOATS

The American photographer backed his MG Midget close to the wall, got out of the car, up onto the trunk lid, and jumped—landing chest and stomach in the ivy that covered the top of the wall; he sat up as if he were on a horse, and was just going to jump down on the inside when he became aware of two large Dobermans approaching among the trees.

He had arrived in Geneva the day before yesterday. Rumors of a mysterious Hispano-Suiza had brought him there. A few weeks before, he had visited Michael Sedgewick in Midhurst, a small town a couple of hours drive south of London. Michael had told him about the magnificent Hispano-Suiza he had seen by coincidence in Geneva a few years ago. Collectors and experts were not aware of this car, Michael said, and the owner never showed it to anyone. He just mentioned it in passing, as an intriguing story, but the American photographer made him reveal the address. Michael had shaken his head and said that one had to be a king in exile to get into that place, and that he had better forget about this Hispano-Suiza.

Sitting on the wall, seeing the two dogs coming closer, the American photographer felt inclined to agree with Michael. Yesterday he had tried to locate the phone number so he could make an appointment with the owner, but there was no phone listed under that name. He then decided to drive out to the house. He asked several people for directions, and they had all heard of it. Before the present owner moved in, it had belonged to an oil millionaire whose name he had seen often in the gossip columns. The American photographer drove north along the shore of Lake Geneva until he found the house. He became very discouraged when he saw the high walls and the tall iron gate. He tried to open it, but it was locked. There was just no way he could communicate with the people inside. He was ready to give up. Then, after thinking about how much he had sacrificed to come this close to an undiscovered Hispano-Suiza, he decided it was worth taking a wild chance.

The American photographer forced himself to jump down before the dogs came any closer to the wall. He stuck his hands in the coat pockets; it made him look more casual, and it also protected his hands from the dogs in case they attacked. They showed their teeth and growled, but didn't bark. He stopped and talked to them in his most soft and inviting voice. They came slowly up to him, showing possible signs of affection. First they sniffed on his pant legs, then they jumped up and tried to lick his face; the ice was broken.

Relieved, the American photographer continued towards the house, where he found the gardener. He handed him a business card and pointed in the direction of the house. The gardener nodded, cleaned his hands on his overalls, took the card carefully by the corner and then started walking towards the main building.

Three days after this adventure in Geneva, the American photographer arrived in Monte Carlo. Now he was relaxing in a comfortable chair on the eleventh floor sun deck of a high-rise apartment overlooking the Yacht Harbor of that fashionable resort. Yves-Jaques Rey-Millet, the young owner of the Hispano-Suiza, sat in the chair beside him, listening to his experiences in Geneva.

It had taken ten minutes or more before the gardener returned, with a blond, Scandinavian-looking girl. She had listened to what he had to say, and then explained that the owner of the Hispano-Suiza had recently moved to Monte Carlo. It was the brother who lived in the house now. She promised to send a telegram arranging a meeting in Monte Carlo. The car was still in the garage in Geneva, and he saw it in all its splendor before saying goodbye, going through the gate this time.

(Continued overleaf)

This was the sight that met Yves-Jaques Rey-Millet when he turned the spotlight on a dark corner inside his grandfather's boathouse. The small picture above shows how trees had started to grow in the driveway of the abandoned building where the rare automobile had been hidden since the outbreak of World War Two. The Hispano-Suiza was remarkably intact under the layers of dust. The tires were removed during the years when rubber was a sought-after commodity, and the beautiful ornament that crowned the radiator had been stolen by some dishonest enthusiast. The owner is still looking for it; he won't settle for anything less than the original.

GE·73737

Casually parked on the cobblestone yard of a 17th-century castle outside Lucerne, the Hispano-Suiza displays its elegant lines. The original body was created by Kellner of Paris, while the restoration was done by Philipinettis in Geneva. Today it looks like it did back in the Thirties, when Jean-Jaques Rey-Millet's grandfather used it for his frequent trips from Paris to the summerhouse outside Bordeaux. He insisted on driving himself, leaving the chauffeur to take care of parking and polishing. Grandmother insisted on not knowing what was going on—during those wild drives through the French countryside, she pulled the curtains around her, in the back seat.

Yves-Jaques laughed about the Dobermans. They were no good as watchdogs, he complained. He leaned back in the chair and closed his eyes, letting the afternoon sun warm his face as he began to recall how the Hispano-Suiza was discovered.

"I first heard about it from my grandmother. She remembered that before the war grandfather had owned this incredibly expensive car. It was beautiful, she said. He had bought it new in 1934. They lived in Paris then, and he had a chauffeur drive him around in the city. I wish I could have seen him coming up the Champs-Elysee in that elegant car. On the week-ends, when they used it for their trips to the summerhouse outside Bordeaux, he always insisted on driving it himself, leaving the chauffeur to take care of parking and polishing. He used the car until 1939, when he realized what was happening in Europe, and moved to the United States. The car, grandmother thought, was hidden in the boat storage building at the summer house. But she wasn't sure. Nobody had been there for at least twenty years.

"I chose my Lamborghini Miura for the trip to France, and asked my friend Pierre to join me. We left early in the morning from Geneva, and hoped to be in Bordeaux before dark. But it started to rain outside Bergerac. It poured down, in fact! It must have been close to eleven o'clock in the evening before we arrived. By then I was extremely eager to see if the car was there. The caretaker, an old woman who had lived there since before the war, had been warned about our arrival, but she certainly didn't expect us this late. We knocked on the door. After a long time, we felt, the door was opened, reluctantly. When I saw her bent back and tiny body, I realized how anxious I must have been. Imagine, awakening this poor old lady in the middle of the night! I was embarrassed, but it was too late to turn back now. I asked if she could show us the boathouse tonight. She didn't look happy, but went back into the house and returned with keys and flashlight, dressed in a big wrinkled raincoat. It was still pouring down.

"We fumbled with the key in the darkness trying to open the gate. It was obvious that it hadn't been used for many years. Trees had grown up in the middle of the driveway behind the gate. We finally got it open, and eagerly continued over to the boat-

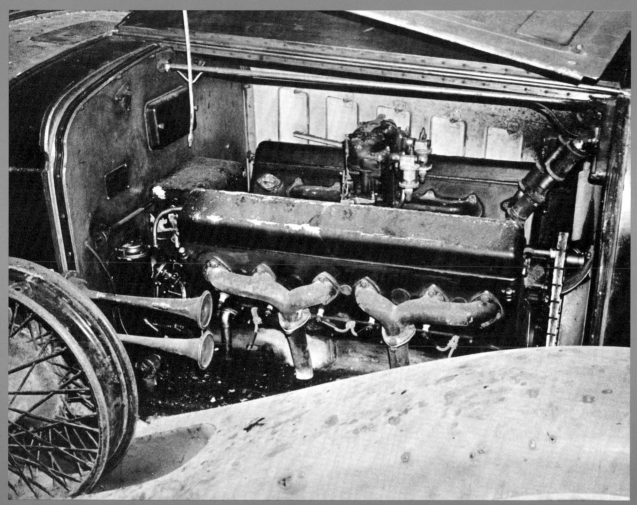

Pictured above is the magnificent power source of the Hispano-Suiza. The photograph shows the eleven-litre V-12 engine, the way it looked when it was found. Very little had to be done to restore it to original working condition; not even the fan belt visible in the picture had to be changed. The photograph on the left-hand page shows the true coupé-de-ville bodystyle, with its separate passenger and chauffeur compartments. Notice the removable hardtop over the driver's seat—no wonder the owner preferred to drive the car himself.

house, the old lady lagging behind. We got that door opened, too, and stumbled on each other's feet trying to get under the roof. It was still pouring down.

"A strong odor met us; a mixture of salt water, tar and rotting wood. I asked for the flashlight. I remember the beam cutting through the thick darkness, as I moved the light quickly around the room, which was filled with boats and garden furniture. I saw the car almost immediately. It was sitting on its rims over in the corner. I stumbled again as I walked closer, this time on a canoe lying beside the car. I let the light shine on the radiator. It showed a badge with a pair of wings, but no name. I opened the bonnet. It said Hispano-Suiza, on a brass plate.

"I hurried back to the house, and placed a long distance call to Claude Sage in Geneva. He was the director of Philipinettis who specialized in restoring vintage cars. He sounded very sleepy when I got him on the line. It must have been past midnight. I explained what I had found. He asked how many cylinders it had. I had forgotten to check! He told me that if it was a V-12, it was extremely rare. Only 127 were built, and no more than thirty were known to remain today in the entire world. I asked Claude to wait while I ran back to check. I had to know right away! It was still pouring down.

"Back in the boathouse I opened the bonnet again and moved the flashlight from sparkplug to sparkplug as I counted them. It was six. I was disappointed. Then I suddenly remembered that Claude had talked about a V-engine. I opened the bonnet on the other side. There were six more! I rushed back to the phone. Claude seemed to be just as excited as I was. Pierre asked the old lady if she had anything we could celebrate with. She opened a cupboard and found a bottle of red wine, but she didn't seem to appreciate the occasion."

The Hispano-owner and the American photographer shook hands. They had decided to meet in Geneva in two weeks to photograph the car. As the photographer entered the street below, the yachts were coming back into the Harbor after a day on the sun drenched ocean. He looked up to the eleventh floor of the tall building above him. Yves-Jaques was enjoying the scenery through his binoculars.

A DIFFERENT TALE OF THE UGLY DUCKLING

He had been driving all day with this noise. Early in the morning, after he left Munich, he had become aware of the new unfamiliar sound that had been added to all the old familiar sounds of his MG Midget. It was very subdued in the beginning. In fact, he was listening to it while he was driving, and he was sure it was there. At other times he couldn't hear it, and he was sure it wasn't there. When he passed Memmingen there was no longer any doubt. It was there. Did it come from the engine, or from the transmission, or from one of the wheels? He couldn't tell. It sounded worse, the closer he came to Bodensee.

When he stopped for passport control in Lindau, on the border between Germany and Austria, the noise sounded very serious, but he decided to continue in spite of that. He wanted to reach Zurich before the end of the day. He had several important appointments there, with owners of Bugattis and Alfa Romeos.

On the highway, when he was making sixty, he couldn't hear the noise any more, or maybe he was only getting used to it. He had just crossed the Swiss border, and was approaching a town, when suddenly there was a terrible sound of metal grinding against metal. It came to a violent climax, then everything was silent. He pressed the accelerator, but nothing happened. He coasted down the last hill to the town, and there was just enough speed to roll up in front of a gas station. The American photographer was very depressed. Was this the end of a trip that had started out so well three weeks ago? He didn't even know where he was, and asked the station attendant. The name of the place was St. Gallen.

Mister Albin Machaz lived in this town. He was a creator of fabric patterns. He usually spent most of the day in his studio at Stoffels, wrestling with the designs for next year's collection. But this particular day in the autumn of 1950, he had to take his Citroen to the garage in St. Margarethe Strasse to be serviced.

As he waited for his turn to discuss with Fritz, the owner of the garage, what needed to be done to the Citroen, he saw a little sports car in the corner by the wall. From the way it was parked, he got the feeling that it had not been driven there under its own power. It looked like it had been pushed into that awkward position. He walked over to it. The colors were bright red, with beige upholstery. It was a two-seater, with very small doors. The wire wheels were large. Too large for the car, he thought. There was a strange combination of styling elements, as if things had been added to the original design. Basically it looked like the race cars he remembered from the late twenties, but the front fenders and the curved grille reminded him of the way the cars looked just before the war. What was it? He walked around to the front. It said Monza Grand Prix. Mister Machaz had never heard of it. He bent over and placed his face close to the radiator grille, to see what was behind it. There was another name plate in there. He moved his hands to shadow his eyes from the sun, but he couldn't read what it said. Fritz was coming over to him.

"Fritz, what is this thing? I have never seen anything like it in my whole life."

"I have no idea, Albin. A young bearded fellow pushed it in here a couple of months ago. He said he thought the engine was blown. I looked at it. Never seen an engine like that. Supercharged too. I told him it would take months before we would even find out where to get the spare parts. He was a student and he said he had to continue. He had driven it all the way from Sweden, and now he had no travel money left. He said he didn't want the car any more. I didn't want it either, but he was very desperate, so I gave in and bought it. Why, I don't know. I don't know what to do with it. I had it advertised, but nobody wanted it. Maybe I'll put in that Fiat engine I have, over there. Why don't you buy it, Albin!"

"No, no, I've had enough of old cars."

"But you would look very good in this car, Albin! You are an artist. Artists can be crazy. They can drive old cars. You can have it for eight hundred francs."

"What would I do with it? I can't work on cars. I don't even know what an engine looks like inside."

"Albin, you can collect it! It would fit right in with your collection of everything else. I'll give it to you for six hundred and fifty francs."

"I wouldn't take it even if you went down to five hundred."

"Alright Albin, five hundred francs."

"Alright, I'll take it then."

Later that same year Mister Machaz talked to his friend Zollikofer, and persuaded him to take a look at the car. He was an artist also, but his specialty was engines. He found that two cylinders were cracked, and that the linings had really taken a beating. He bored it out to twelve hundred and fifty cubic centimeters; it had been eleven hundred. He made new pistons and fitted two new Solex carburetors; there had only been one before. Zollikofer felt it would run better with two. He also put in an electric fuel pump; before, the pressure created by the higher location of the tank had been enough. But that system would not be able to supply gasoline for two carburetors. That's all he did. It ran beautifully.

Mister Machaz was glad he didn't have to spend more to get the car going. When spring arrived the next year, he took it on a long trip. He went through the Gotthard Pass, and down around Lago di Como and back again. He had no problems with the car, except the discovery that it used a great deal of oil, almost a litre every four hundred kilometers. Maybe that's why there was an exterior oil tank, mounted on the left side. There was also another problem. He noticed that people would turn around and laugh at the car when he drove by. He didn't like that at all.

As time passed, Mister Machaz became more and more interested in his two jumping horses. One was German, the other one was Irish. He enjoyed the horses. Nobody laughed at them. He drove the car only once a month, so it wouldn't deteriorate from just sitting there. He felt that maybe, some day, it would be worth something. But for the moment he was more interested in his horses.

All these years Mister Machaz didn't know what a
(Continued overleaf)

Original photographs of the Rally are very rare and hard to locate; so difficult that owner Albin Machaz had to rely on a small drawing of the car when he restored it. The pictures featured here were found in the archives of the Montagu Motor Museum in England. They show a car with English license plates and a Brooklands-style exhaust system. The event, according to handwriting on the back of the photograph, was Amershati Hill Climb.

Holding the wheel with steady hands, Albin Machaz in the picture above guides his Rally through the curve. The photograph to the right shows a close-up of the water temperature gauge, crowning the radiator. This was an important instrument to keep an eye on in the vintage days of motoring. In the large picture further to the right, the brass radiator makes an attractive focusing point. The small picture to the far right shows the owner in his most aggressive pose, ready to attack a Swiss mountain road.

treasure he had in his garage. Under the shell of faked fenders, grille, and layers of paint, was a most unusual French sports car. It was a Rally Grand Sport from 1928, imported to Switzerland by a certain Mister Sarasin in 1931. It was built in Paris by Eugene Affovard Asniére. It had a four-cylinder Chapuis-Dornier engine, which produced seventy horsepower, and a top speed of one hundred and seventy kilometers. Only fourteen, or maybe sixteen, were ever built, and only two were still known to exist in Europe. The third one lived a forgotten life in Mister Machaz's garage until, one day not too long ago, he was visited by six men from the automobile club. They had heard of the car and wanted to find out what it was. After a very careful inspection, they all agreed that it was a real Rally.

Mister Machaz now felt it was time to restore it to its original condition. He went back to his friend Zollikofer, and together they planned what should be done. The engine and the drive train they would not touch, except for exterior cleaning and polishing. Everything else would be taken apart and stripped down to the metal, and then painted in French racing blue. At one time there were seventeen hundred parts to keep track of in his small garage. Mister Machaz was very enthusiastic. He made up a daily routine, going to his studio early in the mornings, and going home in the afternoons to work on the car. Almost every detail of it was in original condition, once the added parts were taken away. However, they had to make new fenders, relying on old, blurred photographs when they designed them. Mister Machaz was very pleased when, eight months later, the car once again looked like it did in 1928.

The American photographer had been very lucky, after all. The very first evening after that depressing experience with his car, he met Andreas, just by coincidence. Andreas knew both Mister Machaz and Rudi, who had an auto repair shop. Andreas put the American photographer on the tracks of the Rally, and while that car was being photographed, the MG was repaired. Four days after his unfortunate arrival in St. Gallen, the American photographer was on his way again, richer to the extent of sixty pictures of a rare Rally.

The photographs above and far left show why owner Albin Machaz had such a hard time figuring out what kind of car he paid 500 francs for. These pictures were taken in 1950 when the Rally returned from engine restoration. Notice the grill that had been placed in front of the original radiator. The words Grand Prix Monza had been attached to the grill, making identification even more difficult. The picture to the left shows the Rally during the restoration process. At one time over 1700 parts were spread all over the small work area in Mr. Machaz's garage.

DELAGE

A STORY OF CARS AND CAVES

If someone had wanted to find Pierre Strinati this particular day many years ago, it would have been an almost impossible task. His hideout had no address. There were no roads leading to it. There were no houses close by. The nearest phone was miles away. Not even someone familiar with the exact location would have found him, unless this someone would have been willing to risk his neck going down sixty feet in a vertical shaft just wide enough to squeeze through. He would have had to use an expert climbing technique in order to be able to penetrate the shaft. With his back pressing against the limestone wall behind, hands and feet pushing against the wall in front, he would have had to slowly slide down, foot by foot. When the bottom was reached and the shaft turned into a horizontal passage, he would have had to continue another two hundred feet crawling on his stomach. And there he would finally have found Pierre, all alone in the cold and humid darkness of the cave. Only a handful of men possessed the courage and experience to handle such a task. Pierre really was unreachable.

Fortunately, nobody needed to get in touch with him. Before he left on his expedition he had taken care of everything in connection with the operation of the department stores he owned in Geneva and Luzerne. If anything serious had come up, it would have been handled by his staff. If they had been unable to take care of it, the matter would just have had to wait until he returned. Officially he had left on a business trip, but his close friends knew that he

(Continued overleaf)

The rare photograph on the left-hand page is from
the 1938 Paris Auto Show, and features some of
the cars displayed by Delage. The light car in the
bird's view is the new model for the coming year.
It differed only in minor details from the model of
the year before. The picture above was taken just
after the Delage was delivered to Pierre Strinati by
Graber himself, the famous coach builder. Pierre had
seen the car on his way back from a cave expedition,
and immediately decided it was the car for which
he had been searching so long. With lines like these
it is easy to understand why the owner rates it the
most beautiful among the cars in his collection.

X

Early morning sun melting away the mist over Lake Geneva, as the beautiful Delage was driven up to the water's edge. Passers-by on their way to work stopped for a moment to enjoy the scene from a long-gone era. Owner Pierre Strinati, in the picture to the far left, was answering questions from the curious, while keeping a steady eye on the imaginary road in front of him for the benefit of the photographer. The large picture on the left-hand page shows one of automobile history's longest bonnets, looking even more impressive through the camera's wide-angle lens. The photograph to the near left captures the forms of fender and bonnet, the elegant flowing lines interrupted only by the powerful-looking exterior exhaust pipes. The Delage name badge, in the small picture above, appeared on this car for almost the last time. It was created at the beginning of the century, surviving World War One but disappearing after World War Two, when Delage made an unsuccessful attempt to regain its market in a changed world.

had taken a week off to work on his doctor's degree in Zoology. The title of his dissertation was "The Cave Animals of Switzerland."

He was resting on knees and elbows. His face was very close to the ground. The headlamp attached to his World War One helmet made only a small circle of light as he was going over every inch of the ground. He was searching for insects, the very special ones only found in caves. They belonged to the families of spiders and crickets and other kinds of insects common in the world outside the caves. But in the caves they were blind. Where the eyes should have been, there was nothing. And they were color-less.

When he found an insect, he would open his shoulder bag and reach for the wooden box that contained brushes and tubes filled with alcohol. He would take a small brush, dip it in alcohol and place a drop on the insect, pick it up with tweezers, study it for a moment to evaluate his find, and then put it in one of the tubes. When he came home he would examine it carefully. During his cave expeditions he had discovered several species that were unknown to man; insects that had never been viewed by an eye. This research was his main interest; the interest over-shadowing everything else. Except for one other thing.

He sat up with his back against the wall to rest for a while and adjusted the headlamp so it would shine straight down in front of him. Then he picked up a small steel bottle from the bag, twisted the cap open, turned it around and filled it with the golden brown content of the bottle. It was French cognac. He took only a mouthful and swallowed it. The unbelievable physical and mental demands on a cave explorer could only be understood by someone who had experienced them. There were the physical hardships by the low temperature, the humidity, the inaccessi-bility. And the mental hardships caused by the total darkness, the closed-in space, and the loneliness. A man could go crazy in the caves.

Now when he rested he realized how tired he was. He had been in the cave for three hours, not counting the time it had taken to climb down. He leaned back against the wall and felt the burning sensation of the cognac finding its way to the stomach. He was

relaxed now, and he found it pleasant to let his thoughts wander into his other field of interest: cars. Not just any cars, but the special cars that he liked.

During the last decade preceding World War Two, the mechanics of the automobile had been refined, resulting in increased performance and reliability. Body styling had also undergone an evolution. From the primitive forms of the early beginnings, via the utilitarian elegance of the vintage years, the designs had now become extravagantly decorative. These were the cars that Pierre preferred, and collected.

His left leg was getting stiff. He shifted position and turned off the headlamp. After all he was going to rest and think for a while now and it was important to save the batteries. He was always worried about running out of power. He returned to thinking about cars. After the war had started many car-makers were forced to convert their plants to war-production. Other makes simply ceased to exist as their markets suddenly disappeared. When the war was over it took several years to raise capital and rebuild factories. These events had created a gap of almost a decade. During this period virtually no civilian cars were built. Pierre turned these facts around in his mind and concluded that the cars of 1948 could just as well have been the cars of 1940. He thought about how few people shared his feelings for the cars from this era. The majority of car enthusiasts were excited about the horseless carriages. An increasing number were of course attracted to the vintage cars, but very few appreciated the cars from the immediate prewar and postwar periods from a collector's viewpoint. But pierre was not going to worry about that. He knew what he liked.

He sank deeper into his thoughts. They began to take the form of pictures. He saw the large garage he had built for his collection of cars. He saw it in the sun among the fruit trees and wild grass on the lot behind the house his father had owned. From there he could see out over Lake Geneva. It was a beautiful spot for a garage. Worthy of the beautiful cars it housed. In his thoughts he started to move along the rows of cars in the garage. There was the Bugatti 57 C, then the Horch with its chromed streamlined headlights, the little round BMW 328, the Talbot

Lago Grand Sport which was one of the last ones made, the Talbot T 150 C, the Lagonda V-12 designed by W. O. Bentley, the Jaguar SS 100, the Ferrari 212, the elegant Lancia Astura, the Maybach SW 38. He thought of how much time he had spent on trying to find a Maybach Zeppelin. He had finally been forced to give up and he purchased the SW 38 instead. Then he moved on to the dark blue Mercedes-Benz 540 K, the Delahaye 135 MS, the Talbot C SS, the Bugatti 57 that had been a convertible but now was rebuilt to a coupe. This was the car he used for every day driving for many years. Then there was the ugly Voisin which was one of the last ones built. And then came the Alfa Romeo 8 C 2900, the Aston Martin DB 2, the Maserati A 6 1500, the Pegaso Z-102, the Mercedes-Benz 300 SL and the BMW 507 he had purchased new at the Geneva Salon some years ago. This was another car he was using when he didn't use the Land Rover.

But there was one missing; a car he had wanted for a long time now. The Delage D 8-120. It was probably the most beautiful car of the prewar period. He knew it was a subjective opinion of course. I must take time to stop at Grabers on my way back to Geneva, he thought. They had supposedly found a Delage in perfect condition.

He suddenly realized how cold he was. He must have been sitting there too long. He must break the thought-fixation before it was too late. Your mind could do strange things to you in a cave. He forced himself to turn on the light again, and adjusted the cable from the headlamp following it down to the breast pocket of his overall where the batteries were. Everything was in order. He screwed the cap back on the bottle and returned it to the bag. The watch on his left wrist showed ten till two. The one on his right wrist was one minute faster.

He was eager to finish this cave now. Just ten more minutes and he would start climbing up. He thought about the strange insect he had found earlier this morning. It looked like a scorpion, but it had no sting tail. The body was covered with hair. He wanted to get back home and examine it. Maybe it was another undiscovered species. And he was eager to see the Delage. Maybe it was the one he had been hunting for so long.

Pictured to the left, is Pierre Strinati as a cave explorer. The cave entrance in the background is found near Montraux in Switzerland. The picture was taken during an early expedition, when Pierre still wore his old World War One helmet. Today he uses a not so nostalgic, but much lighter plastic helmet. The photograph above features another of the over twenty classics in Pierre's private collection—the famous Jaguar SS 100 from 1939. The car has an exceptionally attractive one-of-a-kind body.

BENTLEY

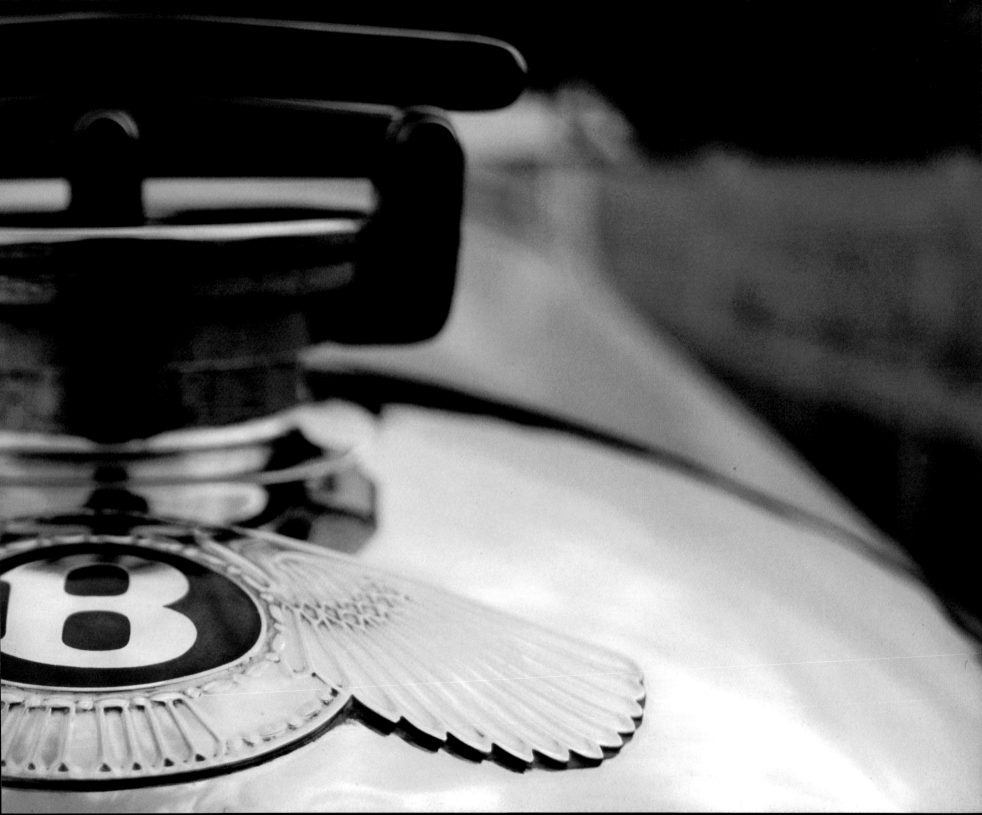

GRANDFATHER WITH THE TASTE FOR SPEED

Bob May hoisted himself from the sofa. As he stood up and started to walk towards the huge fireplace at the end of the living room, the American photographer noticed how tall the Englishman was. He must have been six foot four; maybe even six foot six. He was a big man. And he was the kind of man who didn't seem to have any problems in life. He always had a smile on his lips. When he talked he would end the sentence with the corners of his mouth half way up his cheeks, and the wrinkles around his eyes would make them look like big happy prunes.

Bob didn't seem to care much about how he looked. His pants were too wide and they were baggy and unpressed. His hair was not combed in any particular style. It looked like it had a will of its own. And Bob wasn't able to do anything about it, except that he occasionally ran his big hand through the gray mane, forcing it straight back.

He returned to the sofa with an enormous trophy under one arm, and a stack of photographs under the other. The trophy was beautifully ornamented and topped off with a lady that looked like a winged relative of the Statue of Liberty. He dropped his load of pictures on the floor and sat the trophy down carefully on the coffee table.

Back on the sofa he pulled out his glasses, placed them on his nose, and picked up an old faded photograph from the stack on the floor.

"This is the first picture I have of myself with a car. It's a Lancia Lambda. Italian job. I bought it for eight pounds. I was sixteen then, if I remember right. My first car."

He handed the picture to the American photographer who looked at it for a moment and then asked teasing questions.

"What about the bouquet of flowers you are holding here? And what about that smile? Were you asking for your girl friend's hand?"

"You are almost right. That picture was actually taken by my girl friend. I came racing up the road to their farm and spun an impressive circle in the yard in front of the house. When the dust had settled I saw her running towards me, calling me names. She was rather angry. That's when I pulled out the flowers. She thought that was so nice, so she wanted a picture of me and the car. I had a lot of fun with that car. And it was very fast. Sold it for one pound."

He laughed and sorted out some more photographs and lined them up in front of the sofa, leaning over them as he continued to talk.

"These pictures are from some of the speedboat races my son and I took part in. I started racing them more than twenty years ago, and when my son got old enough, he joined me as a co-driver. In the beginning it was just for fun, but we got more seriously involved, bought a better boat, and became a pretty good team, if I may say so myself. We competed every year in the Paris Six-Hour-Race held on the Seine River. It was always a tough race. The average speed was around 60 mph. The best we ever did was ninth. Our worst race was the last one, when our boat sank as we drove out for start. Very embarrassing. But I'm real proud about our two victories in the only 24-hour races ever held in England."

The American photographer had met Bob May for the first time a few days earlier. That was at the "Brooklands Reunion" in London. Bob had been there with his beautiful Bentley. The American photographer asked him about it.

"You see, when I turned fifty-five, I said to myself,
(Continued overleaf)

The picture on the left-hand page shows a Bentley Speed Six on the banking at Brooklands outside London. The driver takes a fast test lap without wearing his head protection. Notice how the inside front wheel is several inches off the ground. The photograph above was taken during the 1929 Le Mans race, when Bentleys captured the four first places. In the picture to the left, legendary Bentley driver and financier Captain Woolf Barnato and co-driver Jack Durfee enjoy the sweet taste of success after winning the six-hour race at Brooklands in 1929.

wner Bob May, in the picture above, makes himself comfortable behind the wheel in his Bentley. He wears the old driving gear that has stayed with him for so many years. The glasses are the ones he bought right after the war, to wear when riding his motorcycle. Then he used them for speedboat racing, and later they followed him to vintage car events on three continents. In the picture to the left he takes off for a fast drive through the English summer landscape. The Bentley badge makes a natural center point in the symmetrically composed photograph on the left-hand page. Autocar artist Gordon Crosby designed the famous badge.

'Now it's time for you to take it easy and enjoy life. No more speedboat racing. No more working.' I had turned my little carpet store into a big business through the years, and now I felt my son could take over. So when a life insurance matured I thought I would just sit around, take life easy, and live off the money. That's when I happened to run into this Bentley. When I saw it, I felt it was one of the most attractive cars I had ever seen.''

''So that's where the insurance money went?''

''That's right. Every bit of it, and a little more. Later I went to see old W. O. Bentley himself. This was just before he died. When I told him how much I had paid for it, he said that if he had received that kind of money for his cars back in the Thirties he would never have gone broke.''

''So now you just sit around?''

''No. No. I can't sit still, I guess. I have been active all my life. But I did quit the speedboat racing. And I don't go to the office much anymore. The Bentley takes all my time.''

He looked through the stack of pictures again and found some of the Bentley.

''This picture was taken in Australia during a vintage rally. From there I shipped the car to Vancouver, Canada. I drove down the coast to Los Angeles, cut across the country and went up the east coast to Quebec, Canada. Quite a trip. This picture is from New Zealand. That's me on the motorcycle there. It's a 1922 AJS. In 1973 I went back to the United States again. I met so many wonderful people there. All of them were Bentley owners. This year I went to South Africa. Took part in the Durban-Capetown Rally. Look at this picture here. That's my friend, Ken Revis, my map reader. He's blind. Got his face blown off in a bomb raid on the Brighton Pier during the war. The night before we drive I tell him our route for the following day. And Ken memorizes it. Next day in the race he tells me to go left here, and right over there. Here's a river, and so on. Quite a chap, Ken! Here are some shots from Spain. These are from Scotland, I think. Yes. And these are from Ireland.''

He leaned forward and lifted up the big trophy he had taken down from the fireplace mantel.

''I have a lot of plaques and trophies over there, but this is my favorite. It's called the Musical Watch, why, I don't know. I got it when I won the Garda Veteran Race. We drove on the shores of Lake Garda in Northern Italy. Isn't she magnificent?''

He returned the trophy to the coffee table. His wife had brought in tea with crackers and lox during the conversation. Bob pointed towards the tea and raised his eyebrows in a questioning expression.

''Want more?''

When the American photographer shook his head, Bob stood up and smiled.

''I want you to meet my son and my granddaughter. They live just a few miles from here. We can take the Bentley.''

Looking back on the drive with the Bentley, the American photographer realized that it had been one of those experiences when time had been standing still. It couldn't have lasted more than five minutes, but it seemed much longer. So much had happened. He couldn't believe that a big vintage car with crude steering and shifting mechanisms could be handled so elegantly through the curves, and shifted so smoothly through the gears. He remembered sliding around in the back seat during the fast drive. He had no hands to hold on with; they were needed to operate the camera, since he had decided to record the experience. A long time afterwards he could still remember the flashes of pictures he saw through the camera's viewfinder; trees and stone walls and houses rushing by, strong hands on the steering wheel, meeting cars and gaping pedestrians.

When they arrived at the house they had found Bob's son in the garage working on the restoration of another Bentley. They had talked about it for a while, then they had walked out on the big lawn together, where Bob's Bentley was parked. The granddaughter, only five years old, had come running towards them, her blond hair like the mane on a galloping horse. Bob had caught her in the flight and given her a big hug. Then he had sat her down in the grass, taken off his driving cap and glasses, put them on her little head, and lifted her up behind the wheel. Bob had leaned close to her and asked if she had a taste for speed too, just like grandfather. And his eyes had become like big happy prunes.

Pictured on the left-hand page, is Bob May at the age of sixteen behind the wheel in his first car, a Lancia Lambda. He surprised his girl friend with flowers, and she surprised him with a camera. Later he sold the car for one pound. In the picture to the left Bob enjoys the scenery along the rainy Atlantic coast during a vintage rally in Spain. He was known for driving with the hood down in all weather conditions. This is one of the few occasions when a photographer caught him violating his own rule. The picture above shows Bob May as a speedboat racing ace.

ROLLS-ROYCE

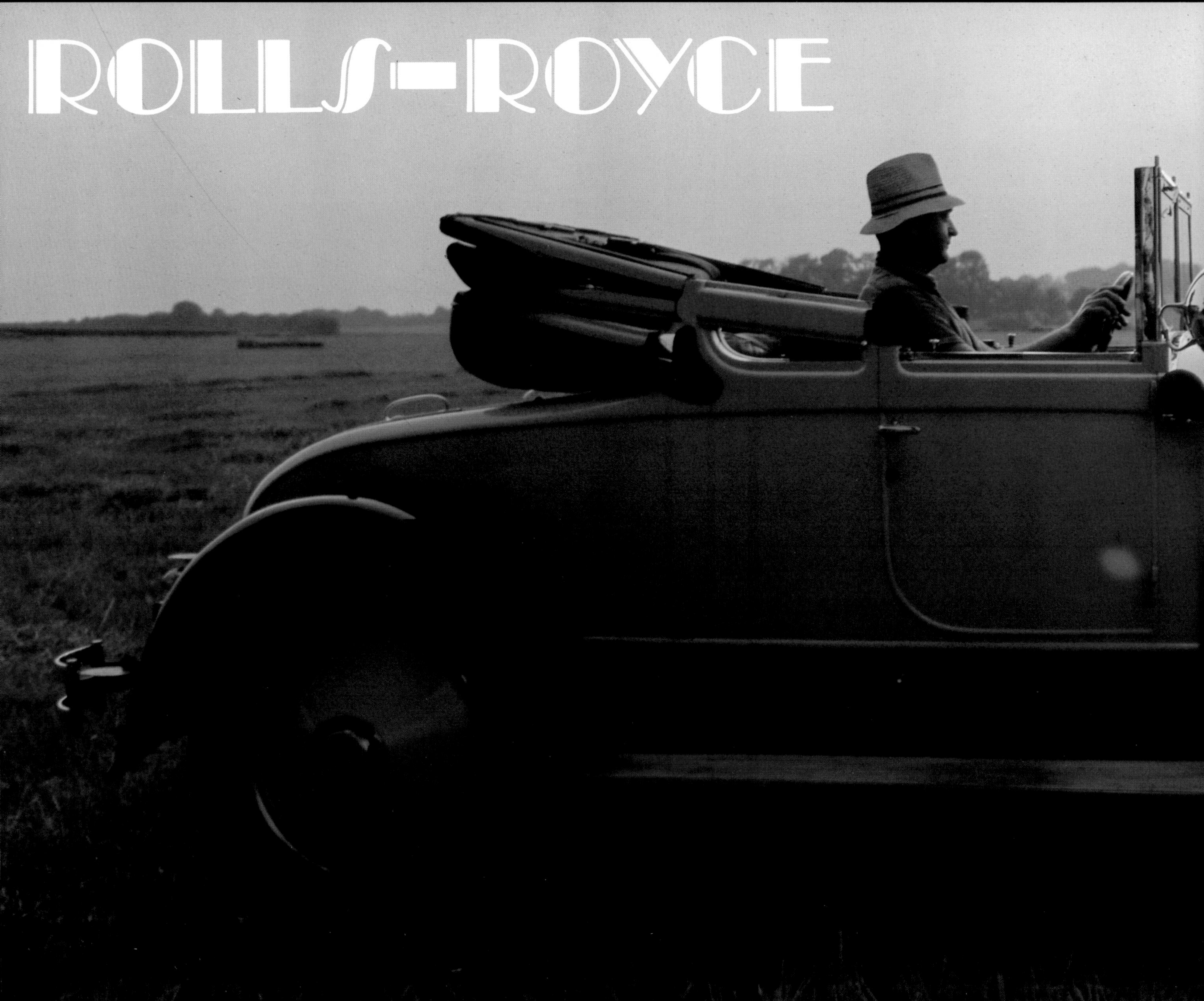

PASSIONATE ENCOUNTER WITH WINGED LADY

A handful of workers were adding finishing touches to the platform they had built for the auctioneer and his staff. It was located half way between two large tents that looked like gigantic sailing ships. The cloth sides were rolled up on the flanks facing the platform. Behind the criss-cross patterns formed by ropes and masts were the rows of vintage automobiles. They had been parked side by side, in the shade under the brown tent roof. It moved slowly in the wind. The cars reflected their elegant bodies in each others' polished surfaces. People were walking up and down between the rows, standing in groups around the cars, bending over details or looking in their auction programs. It was almost time for the auction to start.

Mister Adrian Liddell had parked his Hispano-Suiza among the trees, quite a distance from the actual auction area. As he walked towards the tents, he could feel that it would be a hot day. It was already warm. People around him had taken off their jackets and thrown them over their arms or shoulders. Voluminous cotton clouds were sailing across the blue sky, creating large shadow areas on the English summer landscape as they moved.

The crackling voice of the loudspeaker announced that the auction was now beginning. The first car was driven up with clouds of smoke shooting out from its exhaust pipes. Just as Mister Liddell turned around to join the bidders at the platform, he caught a glimpse of a big yellow car. He felt a quick sting of excitement in his chest. He stopped abruptly,
(Continued overleaf)

The large photograph to the left shows the Rolls-Royce parked outside owner Adrian Liddell's home in Southern England. Beside it is the Hispano-Suiza he used for his trip to the auction where he had his first dramatic encounter with the Rolls-Royce. The small picture above was found in the files at Montagu Motor Museum, and describes better than words the fascinating experience of vintage motoring. The automobile is a Rolls-Royce Phantom I. Notice the solid rims; the same as used on Adrian Liddell's car.

YN 9160

He fell in love with her at first sight!
Owner Adrian Liddell said he felt as if
the most beautiful woman imaginable
had walked into the room—he couldn't
take his eyes off her. When he saw the
yellow Rolls-Royce in the auction tent, he just had to
have her. And everyone who sees this magnificent
automobile today understands what he felt. In these
pictures, she is even more beautiful, illuminated by
the last beams from the glowing evening sun.

causing a couple of passersby to turn their heads in surprise over his sudden action. He walked over to the car.

It was a Rolls-Royce Phantom One from 1926. The body was built by Barker, in the style commonly referred to as a Doctor's Coupe. The fenders were black, the hood and upholstery brown, but the rest of the car was painted in a ripe yellow; even the enormous solid wheels were yellow. The paint was cracked here and there, the leather seats smooth from wear, and the chrome showing marks from decades of polishing. But these signs of age and loving care only contributed to the car's aura of a timeless antique.

Looking at the car from the side, the rounded tail formed an almost perfect quarter circle. It housed a concealed rumble seat. The air intakes located on both sides in front of the windshield were shaped like ship's ventilators. Crowning all this exquisite elegance was the legendary winged lady, on top of the radiator. These details were all beautiful in themselves, and combined into this Rolls-Royce, they formed an irresistible automobile. Mister Liddell felt it like a pain. He didn't quite like what was happening to him; it was as if he had lost his self control.

The auction official stepped into the car and drove it out of the tent. Mister Liddell suddenly realized that it was now the Rolls-Royce's turn to come up for bidding. He was forced to make a quick decision! Was he going to bid, or wasn't he? But he didn't have to decide; his impulses drove him up towards the platform. When he arrived, he saw that quite a crowd was gathering around the car. There seemed to be a lot of bidding activity. He heard the auctioneer's voice.

"Eighteen hundred pounds. Eighteen hundred."

Mister Liddell pushed and elbowed his way up to the front of the crowd. He caught the auctioneer's eye, lifted a finger, and heard the voice again.

"Nineteen hundred by the gentleman just arrived. Now two thousand. Two thousand pounds."

The auctioneer had immediately turned to a bearded man just a few feet away. The man had lifted his hand and quickly pulled his ear lobe. Mister Liddell lifted his finger again and nodded.

"Twenty-one hundred. Twenty-one hundred

pounds. Twenty-two hundred. Now twenty-two hundred pounds."

The episode with the bearded man had been repeated just as last time. Mister Liddell was still driven by his strong impulses, and lifted his hand again in a last attack on his opponent, this time showing all five fingers!

"Now twenty-five hundred. Twenty-five hundred pounds."

A sound of excitement went through the crowd. The auctioneer looked at the bearded man, and when there was no response, he continued to repeat the last offer. He continued for such a long time that Mister Liddell began to feel a growing irritation with him. He also felt the heat of the sun, took off his hat, wiped away the pearls of perspiration on his forehead and felt the sting of excitement again as the auctioneer finally seemed to come to a conclusion.

"Twenty-five hundred. First, second and . . . twenty-six! Now twenty-six hundred pounds."

The auctioneer looked quickly to see Mister Liddell's reaction, but he had already turned his back to the platform in anger and disappointment. He pushed himself out of the crowd. His tension was slowly loosening as he walked with eager steps back to his car. He turned around once and saw the Rolls-Royce return to the tent. He still felt the pain of disappointment as he drove on the grass around the trees out towards the road. He drove into a large shadow from the drifting clouds as he accelerated out on open road.

Almost a decade later Mister Liddell told his experience to the American photographer, who had just finished shooting a series of pictures of the Rolls-Royce. The car had been parked on one of the recently harvested fields of Mister Liddell's 1000 acre farm in Southern England. The two men were on their way back to the farmhouse, driving the open Rolls-Royce, when Mister Liddell came to the last part of his story.

"I drove to the Lindhurst Hotel, where I ordered a big lunch. I felt in need of something to cheer me up, and the good food helped, at least temporarily. I couldn't understand why I would feel such a sense of loss. But I did. I tried to forget about the car. During the drive home that afternoon I forced myself

In the picture to the left, Adrian Liddell charges up a slippery hill just after the start of the Brunton Hillclimb in 1955. The car is a Buckler prototype, powered by a Ford Ten engine. The photograph above was taken during the 1954 Goodwood Sportscar Meeting, where Adrian Liddell won his class in another Buckley prototype. The streamlined Buckley, number 15 in the picture, was very fast but very expensive to race; the brakes only lasted one event and always had to be relined before the next.

to think about other things, and when I arrived at dinner time the Rolls-Royce had left my mind. But it would dramatically re-enter.

As I opened the kitchen door a little man stood up and introduced himself as owner of the Rolls-Royce. He was ordinary looking, dressed in a brown suit, and I remember wondering if it was some kind of practical joke. He had apparently been waiting for quite a while. He said that the bidding had ended just after I had left, and when the auctioneers went to collect from the bearded man, he had not been able to come up with the money. They told the owner that the car was not sold after all. He had noticed me during the bidding and found my name and address in the bidder's register.

He had looked for me in the tents and everywhere, but when he couldn't find me, he drove to my house. He said he was willing to sell the car for twenty-nine hundred pounds. I concealed my excitement and answered that I would not be able to pay more than twenty-five hundred. He said it was quite impossible to accept such a low offer, but I asked him to wait while I went to my study. I opened my safe and took out twenty-five hundred pounds from it. When I returned, I counted up the bills on the kitchen table. As I had suspected, he couldn't resist the temptation of the cash, and the Rolls-Royce changed owners right there and then."

The American photographer wanted to take a few more pictures before the sun disappeared behind the horizon. He asked Mister Liddell to drive down to the house, swing around and come back up the hill, with the lights turned on and going as fast as he could. The American photographer stood ready with the camera in position. He hoped the exposure setting was right because there was not time to reset it between the quick shooting required to capture the car as it passed. There it came, under the big oak tree, with the headlights beaming, throwing up clouds of dust illuminated by the orange light from the low sun. He took three frames as the car approached, managed to take another one as it went by, and a last one after it had passed. The dark silhouette of the Rolls-Royce disappeared into the dark silhouette of trees, leaving only the red brake lights as evidence of its existence.

BUGATTI

DELAYED FOR A DATE WITH A FRENCH BEAUTY

The hot sun was burning his bare chest and arms as he drove his open MG Midget along the coast on the French Riviera. It was stop and go much of the time, but when he had a chance, he let the engine reach its peak in the gears, enjoying the cool draft the speed sent swirling around his body. He had started from Cannes almost an hour ago, and had spent all this time reaching Frejus. The roads were jammed with cars, transporting tourists in their obligatory uniform: sunglasses and bathing suit. They were all eager to reach their favorite spot. The American photographer couldn't see how there would be room for more people on the beaches; they were already packed. He stopped in Frejus to fill up his supply of lemonade, knowing that he would consume a dozen bottles on a hot day like this.

The coast offered breath-taking scenery, with the pine trees growing on the hills, climbing dangerously all the way down to the water, here and there leaving a strip of yellow sand for the waves to have their rendezvous with land. A white haze rested over the ocean, but revealed enough of the Mediterranean Sea to verify the myth of its blue water. The road followed the ups and downs of the hills, and the ins and outs of the shore. It was a very beautiful drive. But very time-consuming. He had an appointment at Paul Ricard Racetrack outside Marseille at three o'clock. He was getting a little nervous.

The American photographer had cut out a piece of the map that covered today's trip and taped it to the dashboard of his MG. His wristwatch hung beside the map on the light switch. St. Tropez, the meeting place for fashionable young vacationers, was waiting for him further down the coast. He had planned to stop there for a while, but a look at the watch convinced him that he had to get over to the Nice-Marseille freeway as soon as possible. He was just wasting his time on this road. Maybe he should go back to Frejus and cut across there, he thought. He turned around.

He was driving on the freeway now, making good speed. He felt much better about his progress; the coast road had been a disaster. According to the map he should turn off at Brignoles, and then continue maybe 20 miles south from there, where he would find the racetrack. He estimated about 45 minutes of driving before he had to turn off the freeway. As he settled down, subdued by the kind of monotonous freeway driving he was used to from California, yesterday's experience in Nice came to his mind.

He had travelled to Nice in the morning, where he had met Monsieur Binda at his office in Rue St. Philipe. Monsieur Binda was a collector of fine cars, specializing in the finest of them all, Bugatti. The American photographer had an exciting idea to propose, involving one of Monsieur Binda's cars, the 1929 Type 35. This was the model raced so successfully by the legendary Louis Chiron. He lived now in nearby Monte Carlo, and was often seen taking his meals at the Hotel du Paris, where he had supposedly started his career as a bellboy at the beginning of the century. The American photographer wanted to take a series of pictures in Monte Carlo of the fascinating Chiron behind the wheel of the beautiful Bugatti. The streets of Monte Carlo were the scene of the famous Monaco Grand Prix, where Chiron and Bugatti had raced together so many years ago.

Monsieur Binda had reacted very favorably to the idea, but there were a couple of problems; the Bugatti was taken apart for its annual overhaul, and Chiron was not in good health anymore. Monsieur Binda knew him well and said that he refused to see visitors. Understanding the American photographer's disappointment, Monsieur Binda offered to let him take pictures of the Bugatti Type 57 that had recently *(Continued overleaf)*

Looking sternly into the camera is the master himself,
Ettore Bugatti, in the photograph on the left-hand
page. He was a genius in his field, and was never
more satisfied than when involved in solving a
mechanical problem. His designs ranged from the
world's smallest watch to the most gigantic locomo-
tive engine. The picture above shows the Type 57
Atalante in traffic somewhere in England. Notice that
the radiator was so low and deeply recessed that it
could not be seen from the side. To the left is the
Atalante the way it was pictured in the sales literature
printed for the Paris Auto Salon in 1937.

Compared for their artistic qualities, few cars would be able to compete with this Bugatti. The design of Bugatti's engines was already legendary, but with the creation of the Atalante, an artistic high point was reached in the coachwork, also. Ettore Bugatti's son, Jean, was the driving force behind this design. The body was built at the factory, so that the whole car was a product of Molsheim. An unusual bird's perspective in the picture to the right reveals the beautiful lines of bonnet and fenders. The long picture further to the right shows how deeply set the radiator was, protected on both sides by the big round fenders. The small picture below captures the elegant curves of the Atalante's tail end. It looks oversized, but seen as a whole with the large front fenders, it comes out well balanced—and it certainly gave the Bugatti a very distinctive look.

been brought back from the United States. But there was a problem with this car too; it was presently on loan to a small museum at a racetrack outside Marseille. Monsieur Binda had offered to call the caretaker of the museum to have him prepare the car. The American photographer had of course been very disappointed when he realized that the Monaco idea wouldn't work out. But by now he was used to emergency changes. He had accepted Monsieur Binda's offer.

The American photographer looked at his watch. It was a quarter till three. He should have been in Brignoles by now. He began to feel nervous again. A sign read St. Maximin. He consulted the map. He had gone too far! And he had to turn around once more. It would be impossible to reach the track on time. After ten minutes of fast driving he was at the Brignoles turnoff, and a few minutes later he passed the little village. He asked a man on a bicycle for the direction, and he pointed to continue on the same road. The American photographer drove for what must have been almost an hour, without finding the track. When he came to the outskirts of Toulon he understood that he was lost. He asked again and was pointed out another direction, which he followed in desperation. He was very nervous by now.

It was ten minutes till five before he finally arrived. The sun was quite low, and there would only be adequate light for another hour. He could hear the race cars circling the track, trying to get in some last practice laps before dark.

The American photographer located the museum and the caretaker. He was in the process of locking up for the day. Fortunately he understood some English, which made it possible for the American photographer to describe in a most heartbreaking way the many misfortunes on the trip. The caretaker continued to lock up the place, not seemingly moved by the story. The American photographer then decided to use a common salesman technique; he just stood there in silence until the caretaker understood that he wouldn't go away until he had photographed the car.

The caretaker used all the words in his limited English vocabulary to express the importance of

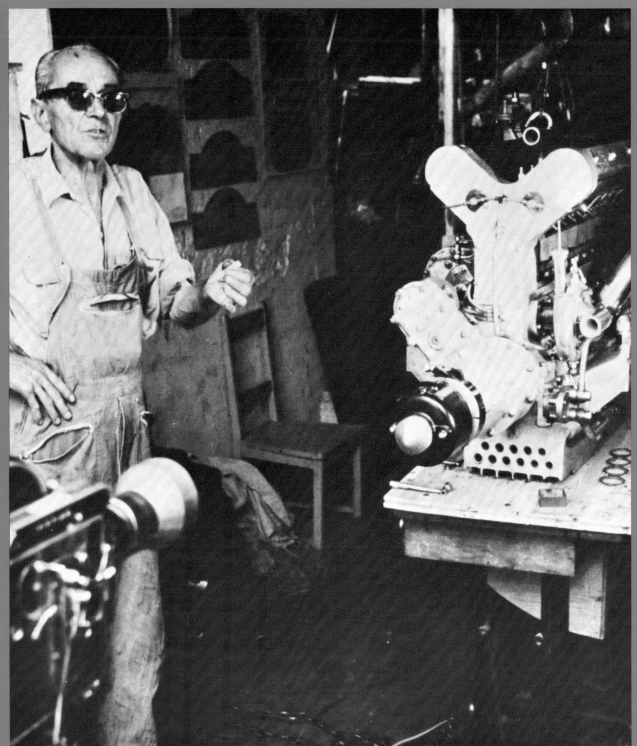

In addition to the Bugatti 57 Atalante featured in this book, owner Andre Binda also has a perfect sample of a Type 35 in his collection. In the picture above, he joins famous racedriver Louis Chiron, to the left, in admiring the legendary race car. The photograph on the left-hand page shows George Lutz, in a pause during his work on the 57-engine. Mr. Lutz was trained in the Bugatti Factory in Molsheim and was later selected to be a mechanic for the Bugatti racing team. Today he works for Andre Binda in Nice, making sure that the cars in the collection are maintained in perfect condition.

locking up the museum right now, but after a few more minutes of the American photographer's persistent silence, he gave up and signaled that he needed help to push the white Jaguar XK 120 out of the way. When he sat down to start up the Bugatti, he remembered that the keys were kept by Monsieur Binda in Nice. He explained that this was another reason he had to lock up right now. But the American photographer started to push and finally the car was outside the museum, with the sun sending its already fading beams down on the Bugatti's dark blue body.

Some fast action was needed now! The American photographer asked the caretaker if he could produce a ladder and some dust cloths. The caretaker's attitude had now changed dramatically and he was very eager to get the whole thing over with in a hurry. He returned quickly with these items and started to dust off the car. In the meantime the American photographer unpacked his camera equipment, attached the lens he had chosen, loaded up with film, and started to move around the car to measure light and look for possible camera angles. Now there was only half an hour of light left.

It hit him like a flash! He realized that he hadn't looked at the Bugatti before now. He suddenly saw how unbelievably beautiful the car was. He had only seen pictures of this model before. But now he experienced the same feelings he had in front of a perfect piece of art. Because the Bugatti was perfect! It expressed it all. Power. Speed. Elegance. He had to force himself out of the spellbinding trance the presence of the Bugatti had put him in.

He began shooting in rapid sequences, working with closeups because of the ugly background. He saw it all through the camera now. The radiator from the side, click. The radiator from the front, click. The badge, click. The radiator cap, click. The headlight, click. He changed quickly to the wide angle lens, and climbed the ladder. He took in the whole car, click. The bonnet with the fenders, click. The back, click. He jumped down from the ladder and stretched out on the ground. He was perspiring. He took the entire front from below, click. The wheel and fender, click. The red of the sun in the chrome, click.

The American photographer continued shooting until there was no more light.

TALBOT-LAGO

THE COUNT GOES TO MONTE CARLO

René turned the steering wheel to the right, accelerated rapidly and gave the clutch a kick to activate the pre-selector gearbox. The long, louvered bonnet of the Talbot-Lago was now pointing west towards Monte Carlo. Other drivers and tourists walking along the busy road were giving the elegant automobile and its passengers curious looks. The distinguished, gray-haired gentleman sitting beside René in the front seat was Count de Wurstemberger, the owner of the Talbot-Lago. The third person in the car, squeezed into the narrow back seat and loaded with heavy camera equipment, was the American photographer. He had a magnificent view from this position. The hood of the Talbot-Lago was folded down, leaving nothing to obstruct the beautiful scenery as it passed by in quickly changing sequences.

The three men had just left the narrow mountain road winding its way down to Menton from Val de Gorbio, where the Count's Riviera villa was decoratively hidden among the park-like vegetation of the six-acre estate overlooking the picturesque valley. The American photographer had arrived from Nice in the afternoon. Later in the evening, he joined the Count and his friend René at the villa. They had been talking for several hours around the dinner table, which had been set outside on the veranda, surrounded by hanging branches and groups of exotic flowers and plants. Earlier in the day the Count had spent some time in the kitchen with the chef, planning the menu for the evening. At the dinner table, they

enjoyed the delicious result: Entrecote with Sauce Bearnaise. They had not talked much during the meal. The Count played one of his favorite records. Cascades of symphonic explosions burst out through the open veranda door, encompassing them with hypnotic power. It was Tchaikovsky.

After dinner, they discussed life in Europe, life in America, life in general, and of course, classic cars. That was the common interest that had brought them together. The Count talked about his experiences as a race driver, beginning with his first race in 1947. In 1954 he had given up racing and left for Africa, where he crisscrossed the jungles in the service of an international pharmaceutical concern. Twelve years later, he returned to Europe. His greatest interest nowadays was his collection of cars. Among these cars he was most attracted to the five Voisins. He admired Voisin's eccentric way of solving technical and esthetic problems. In addition to the Voisins and the Talbot-Lago, he also owned a 1934 MG, a 1936 Rolls-Royce, a 1936 Delage, a 1949 Aston-Martin, and two other postwar classics, both Bristols. Some of the cars were kept here at the Riviera villa, others at the family Chateau in Switzerland. The Count and René were presently engaged in restoring one of the Voisins.

At the end of the discussion, the Count excused himself and left the table. As he walked through the veranda door, leaning on his cane, the American photographer was reminded about what the Count had told him earlier. As a child, he had become the victim of a crippling disease that had left him with a stiff leg. But instead of allowing the handicap to cramp his style, he had developed a proud way of walking. He looked more like a fighter pilot wounded in action. He had that mystical image of a war hero, the American photographer thought to himself. The Count returned with a thick brown envelope under his arm, and suggested that they move inside to the sitting room, where the light was better for looking at the racing pictures he had brought. The air outside had still been warm, and the crickets' monotonous music had taken over where Tchaikovsky left off.

Now the three men were on their way to the Yacht Harbour in Monte Carlo. The American photographer (Continued overleaf)

These photographs describe important phases of Talbot-Lago owner Count Jaques R. de Wurstemberger's life. In the picture above, he is the "race driver." The camera caught him at full speed, driving his HWM on the Bremgarten circuit outside Bern, Switzerland, in 1951. In the picture to the left he smiles happily after having successfully completed the race. The photograph to the far left shows Count de Wurstemberger as the "jungle doctor." The exotic setting was found in Nigeria, where he worked for a pharmaceutical company. The picture was taken in 1958.

No other place could be more appropriate as a setting for the Talbot-Lago than the yacht harbor of Monte Carlo. In the large picture to the left, hotels and apartment high-rises form an impressive background for the elegant automobile. Talbot-Lago was the kind of car that was within the means of the kind of people who anchored their yachts in the famous harbor. Rain would usually be considered a catastrophe by a photographer, but the picture in the middle illustrates how it turned into an opportunity for dramatic expression. The picture above shows owner Count de Wurstemberger carefully selecting a course through the traffic on his way back to the seclusion of his hillside villa.

lifted his camera and placed the viewfinder in position. He was ready to capture the spectacular picture that would emerge before his eyes as soon as the car passed this last curve. There it was, Monte Carlo, magnificent in all its scenic beauty. Modern high-rises and old turn-of-the-century villas were fighting for space as they crowded the shoreline and climbed the steep hills. The entire scene was covered with a soft haze. The American photographer had chosen the Yacht Harbour with the famous skyline behind it as the background for a series of pictures of the Talbot-Lago.

They turned at Casino Square, caught a glimpse of the Hotel de Paris, followed the street to the left and then turned to the right. The Count turned his head so that he could speak easier to the American photographer.

"We are driving on the Grand Prix-circuit now. This curve is called Mirabaux, and this one is the Station Hairpin. There was a railway station here many years ago. The next one is called Portier."

They went straight down to the shore and turned right, following the street as it curved slightly into a tunnel. After the tunnel, when they came out in the sun again, their dazzled eyes were met by the view of the Yacht Harbour with its forest of masts. The Count had been silent in the tunnel, because of the sound from all the cars driving through. Now he continued.

"This is where the chicane is placed. Bandini crashed here in 1967. Terrible accident. We are coming to Virage du Bureau de Tabac. It was named after a tobacconist's kiosk here. Over there is the swimming pool. It was finished in 1973. The cars pass around it and that slows them down. The circuit was too fast for the safety conditions, so these extra curves were added. This is the Gasometer hairpin. Now we are leaving the circuit. We are going straight out along the quay here. This is the point you showed me on the map, where you thought it would be a good place to take the pictures."

René and the American photographer positioned the Talbot-Lago as close as possible to the edge of the quay. It was important to have the car in the right place in relation to the yachts and the water and the skyline. He looked into the camera and shouted short comments to René behind the wheel.

"Two feet back. A little more. That's it. Good."

He was pleased with the way it looked, and took several rolls from different angles. After that, he needed to take it from the back. The car had to be turned around. It would be difficult, as there was very little space to do it on. René squeezed down behind the wheel again. He drove backwards, and forwards, and backwards, and forwards. The steering wheel was very heavy to move when the car was standing still. The engine died several times. It was tuned for fast driving, not for low rev operation like this.

Suddenly there were flames and smoke shooting out from the louvres in the bonnet. René jumped out. It looked like a Le Mans-start in reverse. He opened the trunk lid, found the fire extinguisher, fumbled for a few seconds with the release ring, and then let the white powder spray all over the car. But the flames didn't die. He carefully went closer to the car, and opened one side of the bonnet where the carburetors were. He worked with quick moves to avoid the flames. They shot out even higher now. He sprayed again. This time the flames disappeared. The Count looked terrified, still paralyzed from seeing his prize possession burning. René, with fire extinguisher still in his hands, looked with unbelieving eyes at the mess. The American photographer saw his beautiful pictures go up in smoke. The three men were depressed, to say the least. René opened the other half of the bonnet too. With the lids opened like this, and all white from the powder, the Talbot-Lago looked like a wounded seagull with its wings lifted, trying to fly. It was a pathetic sight.

Just at that point, when they were still gripped by their reactions to the near catastrophe, they felt the first raindrops. In the beginning there were only a few, but soon they came pouring down. The large drops landed with big splashes on the car, mixing with the white powder. René came to his senses first. He jumped back behind the wheel and tried to start the engine. The Count began to fold up the hood. The American photographer cleaned off the radiator and the name badge. He absolutely had to take that shot before he packed up for the day. He looked through the camera viewer. The chrome was spotted with raindrops. Or was it teardrops? To the American photographer, the chances were equal.

These unique pictures are from the first Monaco Grand Prix in 1929. They were found in the files of the Montagu Motor Museum in England. The famous racing event is still held on the same streets of Monte Carlo as it used to be, nearly fifty years ago. The circuit was revisited with the Talbot-Lago during the memorable photo session at this fashionable resort. The large picture shows a big Mercedes-Benz SSK elegantly taking the Gasometer Hairpin. The Talbot-Lago was photographed only a short distance from this famous point. The small picture shows the Mercedes-Benz in the St. Devote turn. Notice the decorative distortion caused by high speed and bad camera lens.

MG

GLADIOLUS TO THE ANONYMOUS WINNER

For hundreds of years, the river Dart in Southern England has been an important waterway. After the sailing ships passed Dartmouth Harbour, where the river became quite wide, they made good speed with their sails full of wind. The sailors on deck could see the small villages of Dittisham and Stoke Gabriel as their ships proceeded further up the river. After the houses of the last village had disappeared in the distance, the river became narrow and it was a slow journey, those last few miles up to the city of Totnes. This was as far as the ships went. On the north shore, there was a warehouse. It was built partially in the water, so that the ships could anchor all the way up to the building when they unloaded their exotic cargoes in the cool and thick-walled warehouse.

The sailing ships are gone today. But the warehouse is still there. Instead of containing Chinese tea, Indian silk and Italian marble as it probably did in the old days, it today houses an exquisite collection of cars and motorcycles.

The American photographer drove his MG Midget up in front of the old warehouse. He had seen the posters advertising Totnes Motor Museum when he passed one of the coast villages on his way from Salcombe back to London. When he came to Stoke Fleming he stopped to make a phone call to the museum. He talked to the owner, explained about the book he was preparing, and made arrangements to meet him here. On arrival, he left the car and went inside.

A nostalgic atmosphere met him. The display area was packed with race cars, sports cars and limousines. It was peaceful and silent in there, but the cars themselves were speaking a visual language, telling of romantic countryside journeys and daring racing adventures. The rough stone walls had been chalked white. The ceiling was held up by an intricate system of heavy beams. The wood had been left untouched, with its gray surface full of cracks and holes, showing the centuries of aging. There were small windows here and there, and a low door, opening right out to the river. Large, old photographs showing race cars and drivers were hanging on the wall opposite the river. The blue body shell of a postwar race car had been mounted on one of the shorter walls. Several old motorcycles hung on the wall facing the river. The cars were placed at an angle out from the walls. In the space between them, there were displays of miniature cars and other car memorabilia. A man and a woman in their early thirties came up to him.

"Are you the American photographer?"

"Yes. And you must be Richard Pilkington."

"Right you are. And this is my wife Trisha."

"Pleased to meet you. My compliments on a very nice collection. And a very tasteful arrangement."

"Glad you like it. Let us take you on a tour."

They showed him all the beautiful cars, stopping in front of every one of them, describing their individual history and features. There were four or five Alfa-Romeos, several Talbot-Lagos, a couple of Frazer-Nashes; altogether about two dozen cars.

During the tour, the American photographer noticed and became very interested in the green MG K3 Magnette. It was the kind of car he was looking for to complete the selection for the book. He asked Richard to tell him more about it.

"The owner is a Swiss calling himself 'Herwe.' He bought the car here in England in 1948. He had to have some modifications made. He had a stiff leg, you see. Among other things the steering wheel had to be detachable, so that he could get in and out of the car. Only thirty-three were ever built like this, with the pointed tail. This particular one is number twenty-four."

"Who was this mysterious 'Herwe'?"

"That was a well-kept secret. He came from a very respectable family, with roots back in medieval history. His forefathers had all been members of the Bern town council. In a conservative society, like the Swiss, it was unthinkable for an aristocrat to be a

professional race driver. So he had to do it under a pseudonym. He was a very good race driver.''

The American photographer pressed himself down in the narrow cockpit. He asked Richard about all the gauges and levers and knobs on the dashboard.

''The brass one to the right of the wheel was used to pump air into the petrol (gasoline) tank. It had a pressure system, you see, and it had to be pumped up both before and during the race. The driver could check the pressure on this gauge here. This is the lever for the pre-selector gear box. You choose in advance the gear you want to use next, and when you want to shift, you just give the clutch pedal a kick, and the gear jumps in. It's a little hard to learn, but once you know the trick it allows for very fast shifting. And that's very important in a race.''

The American photographer placed his right hand on the steering wheel, and his left hand on the pre-selector lever. He tried to imagine how 'Herwe' had felt behind the wheel almost thirty years earlier.

The cars were ready for the start. There were sixteen all in all, placed two and two on the narrow asphalt road. The event was ''Preis der Ostschweiz'' in Erlen, Switzerland. The year was 1948.

Herwe checked the gloves, adjusted the helmet, and loosened his tie a little. It was green with small MG emblems all over it. His beige khaki uniform was clean and pressed. He looked impeccable. It was the way he wanted it.

He looked over the gauges, gave the airpump a few pushes, and checked to see that the pre-selector lever was in first gear. During practice yesterday he had recorded the next fastest lap, giving him the outside position in the first row. His number in this race was twenty-four.

The starter lifted the flag and the sound of the engines increased to a deafening roar as the sixteen cars sped away. Herwe made a good start, but in spite of that he was forced to let Seiler take the inner track in the first turn. They accelerated together out of the curve and Herwe noticed that his own car was faster. On the straight he pushed up alongside Seiler's supercharged MG TC. They drove side by side for several seconds until the next turn came
(Continued overleaf)

The photograph to the upper left captures the MG K3 Magnette in the pits. The wall behind shows some of Herwe's fellow drivers; Rosier won Le Mans in 1950 and Levegh almost repeated the trick in 1952, but the car broke down after he had driven most of the race without a co-driver. The picture to the lower left shows Herwe in the Swiss Alps, practicing for one of the many hill climbs he competed in. In the picture above, two MG race cars are rolling out from the factory in Abingdon. The car to the right appears to be a Magnette, but it doesn't have the pointed tail; the spare wheel is showing, transversely mounted at the rear.

bstinate, aggressive, ferocious—words that well describe the expressive look of the MG Magnette in the picture to the right. The protrusion in the center, below the radiator, is the housing for the supercharger. The small picture in the middle shows the fast-action water filler cap with its decorative overflow pipe and rubber hose. Notice, in the picture below, that the fender is stationary and doesn't turn with the wheel. Headlights and fenders were easy to detach from the body when the car was prepared for racing at Brooklands and similar events. In the side view to the far right, British summer green is attractively matched with British racing green. This photograph reveals the unique pointed tail. Only seven cars with that feature are known to still exist. A picture showing the tail in all its beauty is printed on the last page of the book.

rushing towards them. They both tried to wait as long as possible before braking. Finally Herwe stepped on the pedal and saw Seiler's car shoot out in front of him, braking too late, sliding on the side through the curve, sending sandbags in the air and hitting the safety wall in a cloud of sparks and dust.

Herwe was in the lead now. He held his first position without difficulty until Baer began attacking from behind. He could see the BMW Veritas in the mirror. On the seventh lap it suddenly disappeared as they went out of the Bahnhof turn. On the next lap Herwe saw the car beside the track with the spokes on the rear wheel broken.

He decided to slow down a little, and circled the track in two-minute laps. He had time to send quick glances at spectators and apple orchards around the track. On the sixteenth lap Roos in his red Fiat Mille Miglia showed up in the mirror. But on the eighteenth lap, he too was gone. On the twentieth lap the order was the following: first Herwe in the MG K3 Magnette, second Hirt in the Lancia, third Moos in the MG Super 14.

The situation was the same until the last lap. Herwe, in the lead, was approaching the last turn, fighting hard to keep the Lancia away. He decided to brake very late to have an extra margin when going out of the curve. When he stepped on the pedal there was no reaction. For a tenth of a second he was paralyzed. But then he quickly threw the pre-selector in third, kicked the clutch, threw it in second, kicked the clutch again, and slid around the curve with the tires screaming and the rear end swinging wildly. This unexpected maneuver so startled Hirt that he forgot to take his opportunity to pass. Herwe was quick to open the throttle and accelerated over the finishing line three car lengths ahead of the Lancia.

The spectators came running up to the MG already before it stopped. They were showing their approval of a fantastic race where the fourteen-year-old car had beaten all the postwar ones. A little girl dressed in folk costume was guided through the crowd. She gave him a bouquet of flowers; they were gladiolus.

The American photographer crawled out of the cockpit. He took a few staggering steps to regain his balance. It had been quite an exciting experience.

These photographs were all taken in 1948. In the picture on the left-hand page, Herwe had just passed the finishing line as the winner of the championship race in Switzerland, and his two race mechanics, Jean-Jaques and Vova rushed out to congratulate him. The picture above is from the same race and shows the MG at full speed, on the part of the track that went outside the town. The smaller picture to the left shows Herwe as he accelerates out of the Bahnhof turn. The streets of Erlen were lined with spectators applauding the winning MG, which was fourteen years older than its competitors.

"The Survivors" was photographed, written and designed by Henry Rasmussen. Assistant designer was Walt Woesner. Typesetting was supplied by Holmes Typography of San Jose. The color-separations were produced by Graphic Arts Systems of Burbank. Zellerbach Paper Company supplied the 100-pound Flokote stock, manufactured by S. D. Warren. Litho Craft of Anaheim printed the book, under the supervision of Brad Thurman. The binding was provided by National Bindery of Pomona.